Taste

Taste

A Philosophy of Food

Sarah E. Worth

REAKTION BOOKS

Published by
REAKTION BOOKS LTD
Unit 32, Waterside
44–48 Wharf Road
London N1 7UX, UK

www.reaktionbooks.co.uk

First published 2021
Copyright © Sarah E. Worth 2021

Printed and bound in Great Britain by
TJ Books Ltd, Padstow, Cornwall

A catalogue record for this book is available from the British Library

ISBN 978 1 78914 480 2

Contents

Introduction

When I was a child, I loved Cheerios. I was a pretty picky eater, and so my mother let me eat what seemed to be unlimited quantities of them, since she knew I would at least be eating something. Then one day she told me that if I continued to eat Cheerios at the rate I was going, I was going to turn into a Cheerio. I stopped eating them immediately. I had nightmares of becoming round and having a giant hole in my belly. I panicked. Even at age six, I had internalized the old adage that 'you are what you eat' and that I needed to start seriously considering my diet. I have been thinking about this question of how we are related to our food ever since. In some ways, my diet is still an absolute mystery. I am not at all what I eat. I eat meat and vegetables, and even Cheerios, but I am still a physical person who somehow magically generates consciousness. I have never physically resembled anything that I have eaten, even in the slightest. But what I eat changes my mood, my wakefulness and my energy level. When I eat, however, I literally take inside of me the outside world. I consume (literally), or ingest, that which is not me. That which is other than me becomes me.

In this book I want to begin to tackle some of the questions that develop from our engagement with food and taste. As I see it, when I take in the world outside of me and make it part of me, I am accomplishing something that is truly astonishing. And at the same time, as a philosopher, I do not understand how it is that philosophers have, for the most part, completely neglected this aspect of human experience. The dominant history of Western philosophy has recognized consciousness, minds and the most abstract version of bodies, but not bodies that are hungry, thirsty or craving to ingest. They have not really considered the experience of what it is like to savour a favourite food. Philosophers have long recognized that our bodies need food, water, sleep and sex, but we have a long tradition of approaching these as a distraction from what the *mind* can do: think rationally. We also have a long history of trying to figure out how we, as humans, are different from animals. We take the meaningful difference to be consciousness, language or rational decision-making, but there are a few other aspects that have to do with food which seem important as well. For instance, we are the only species that cooks our food. We are the only ones who dine, rather than just feed. So many human relations are based around gathering, cultivating, cooking, sharing meals and evaluating foods and tastes that I am genuinely surprised that philosophers have not spent more time thinking about it.

One of the world's first gastronomes, Jean Anthelme Brillat-Savarin, said, 'Tell me what you eat and I shall tell you what you are.'[1] Brillat-Savarin had a profound understanding of the relationship between humans and the food we consume. Whether we eat beans and rice, shrimp and grits, or steak and potatoes, our food says a lot about what social class we come from, what part of the world we live in and the cultures from which we come. Tastes are not immune to all of these factors but are largely influenced by genetics, region, religion and class. The writer Adam Gopnik, in *The Table Comes First*, said that we are not what we eat, but it is 'probably closer to the truth to say that we eat what we are: the total self we bring to the table shapes the way we choose, and even how we chew. Our morals and our manners together drive our molars.'[2] This approach broadens what Brillat-Savarin claims, suggesting that *everything* we believe, and all of the ways in which we behave, influence everything about what we eat and how we eat. Manners, preferences and even the ability to cook are influenced by one's thoughts and attitudes about the world. The philosopher Ludwig Feuerbach said frankly, 'You are what you eat.'[3] But Feuerbach's point was deeply materialistic, suggesting that our diet has a direct influence on the health of our brains and thereby our ability to think, and how we invest in the economy, nationalism and the government. Because food cannot be separated from one of the most important economic commodities in our lives, eating is not only a reflection of those economic choices, but literally feeds the brain. Poor food, according to Feuerbach, generates poor thoughts and feelings.

This belief that you are what you eat has been incredibly powerful. It has stayed with us as various cultures have adopted beliefs that we can take on the characteristics of the different animals we eat (there was a lawsuit as recently as 2014 surrounding the slaughter of tigers, because tiger penis was thought to be a great masculinity strengthener).[4] We cannot seem to let go of the belief that dietary fat makes us fat (the so-called lipid hypothesis),[5] and that salt universally raises blood pressure (it does not, unless you have particular underlying health conditions). As it turns out, we do not take on the characteristics of the foods we eat, not even the machismo of tiger penis, and the way that bodies react with different foods, including salt, sugar and fat, all vary so drastically from person to person that it is virtually impossible to make anything other than vague generalizations about them. 'You are what you eat' puts a lot of emphasis on personal responsibility and encourages us to demonize various foods that make us look and feel, we think, not good enough.

Each of these approaches tells us different things about ourselves, our society and our tastes. Each is correct, depending on different disciplinary approaches. What I hope to do in this book is to examine a number of different aspects of eating (taste, recipes, visual aspects, authenticity, cooking and a few specific ingredients) and how some of our latent beliefs about them influence the experience that we often have of eating in a particular culture. I believe that eating is one of the most fundamental things about us as humans and I intend here to add to the understanding of how different aspects of eating can influence the ways in which we think about ourselves.

The whole discipline of philosophy has a bit of a split personality. This could be true in several ways, but what I mean here concerns the deep divide between body and mind. Ever since our earliest ancient philosophical roots, philosophers have talked about the body and mind as if they are distinct, separate and sometimes even mutually exclusive. And the more we *talk*, the more we end up *thinking* of ourselves as distinct entities. The mind (or soul, *psyche* in Greek) is ephemeral and immaterial, but rational and, according to some, immortal. The body is physical, sensual, untrustworthy and sometimes even construed as a burden to the mind. The mind thinks, and is capable of moral reasoning and restraint; the body is passive and its needs and desires can distract us from good thinking. For philosophers, there is no question that the mind is superior.

The locus of concern about the senses for many philosophers involves how reliably we can know the world around us, and the ways in which our minds interpret sensory data. Rationalists, like Plato and Descartes, thought that we could trust only the truths that the mind comes to on its own. They thought that our senses impose an unreliable divide between our minds and the physical world we live in. Empiricists, on the other hand, like Aristotle, George Berkeley and David Hume, thought that we could get reliable knowledge from our perceptions of the physical world through our senses. This debate between rationalism and empiricism has persisted throughout the history of philosophy. Each age brings its own arguments, and of course the reigning science and religion of each era changes many of our fundamental beliefs about human experience. But much of the history of philosophy is dedicated to this fundamental question of how the senses work, and how they can provide knowledge, even if the senses themselves are secondary to particular kinds of knowledge that we like to talk about. Some philosophers do not even discuss the senses when they talk about perception and refer only to the external world and the mind, bypassing the reality of the senses altogether. We tend to think that knowledge only happens in the mind, but the senses are the required negotiator between the mind and the world. Without sensory input, the mind has nothing to contemplate.

Most of what we know about the senses falls under the category of what is called the philosophy of perception, or the 'problem of perception'. Vision is so ubiquitous in the study of perception that when philosophers say perception they almost always mean vision, but all our senses provide information on an unending basis and the input we get from them makes our ability to function possible. Our senses are ranked in order of importance, depending on how well they reliably convey knowledge. Vision is typically the clear winner – so much so that the other senses are often referred to as the non-visual senses. For many, Plato and Aristotle to start with, vision is used as a metaphor for understanding and intellect, as it is located at the front of our head, at the top of our head, and represents what is best about us as humans. Hearing comes in a distant second, and after that, smell, taste and touch are tied for last place. The order of the last three has everything to do with how closely they are associated with the body. Vision and hearing are known as the distal senses because the way they acquire information is not attached to the physical body. Eyes are still part of the physical body, and they can acquire information without having to be in physical contact with the source. Vision and hearing are the principal ways in which we acquire objective, reliable knowledge. Thus when two people *see* an object, they should be able to come up with roughly the same description of the object, whether in terms of colour, length or size. The same is roughly true for hearing. Two people who are in close proximity hear the same tones, words and music. Interpretations of sights and sounds might vary, but the sensory experiences, or sense data, are undeniable. Vision and hearing are so important to gaining knowledge that they are often referred to as the cognitive senses, or the intellectual senses.

The so-called lower senses – taste, smell and touch – are known as the proximal senses since they acquire information literally through the physical body. Vision requires light, sound requires the vibrations of airwaves, but touch and taste both need direct contact with the body in order for sensations to register, and smell usually requires relatively close proximity (although this is also contested). Since we cannot know for certain if two subjects experience the exact same sensations of touch and taste, these senses are less reliable in providing knowledge. Taste often comes in last place in this hierarchy since not only is it tied to the body, but in the process of tasting, we ingest, and so the 'object of inquiry' is literally consumed by the taster. It is destroyed, but it becomes one with the taster.

The lower senses are also more closely associated with pleasure and pain, which are often seen as being completely embodied. Vision and hearing, being cognitive, generally do not produce pleasure in the same way that the body does. If we look at art or beautiful scenery, this is thought to inspire cognitive reflection, but not bodily pleasure. If we taste a favourite dish, it is the physical experience we enjoy. Vision and hearing, although they can both produce cognitive pleasure, do not produce a need to over-indulge. One can be captivated or interested, but it does not happen that when looking at a painting one cannot turn away, such as could happen with a container of ice cream, or with sexual pleasure. Interestingly, taste, touch and smell are not themselves the culprits of gluttony, but it is the body more generally that seems incapable of independent moderation. The body *needs*: it needs sleep, sex, food and drink, and without a rational mind we seem incapable of any meaningful self-regulation. Given this ranking, visual and auditory works tend to be considered more important and to have more cognitive value than works that engage the bodily senses.

This ranking also impacts the social values that are associated with each of the senses. Sight, being king of the senses, is linked with the most important faculty of reason. Vision is said to be the most objective of the senses, and several scholars throughout the ages have said that vision is more important than hearing because one can see much further than one can hear. Hearing was particularly important in the Middle Ages because of the importance that was put on listening to the Word of God. Touch is literally coupled with the body, and is thus regarded as mere physical sensation or *mindless* pleasure. One cannot *know* things through the body, so any sort of experiences provided by taste, touch or smell tend to be considered less important. Parents teach their children visual symbols (like the alphabet and basic symbols) well before they focus attention (if they ever do) on detailed smell identification. But the ability to detect smells accurately can often help with safety in the case of poison or smoke, and before major progressions in medicine, many physicians would smell (and on occasion even taste) patients to be able to detect subtle odours that various diseases tended to produce.

The importance of smell has changed quite a bit over the centuries. Four-legged animals depend on smell much more than humans, developmentally, because they are lower to the ground and cannot see as far as upright humans. But we depend less on smell now than humans have in past ages since we have invented cleaning agents, enclosed septic systems and have considerably higher hygiene expectations. Strong smells are often associated with either food waste or rotting rubbish, or the good smells of cooking. The upper classes were often associated with pleasant smells, perfumes or no smell at all, while the lower classes were associated with body odour, household stench and refuse. Whether or not these stereotypes are accurate is questionable, but the impressions are often still imagined even if they are not real. The upper classes tend to have access to more spacious houses, better cleaning methods and, of course, perfumes. The lower classes are not innately more smelly, but have not always had such easy access to large airy spaces or cleaning essentials for bodies and homes. The sociologists Max Horkheimer and Theodor Adorno suggested that 'vision is associated with the upper classes due to its inherent detachment, while the mingling nature of smell makes it a sign for the "promiscuous" lower classes.'[6] The lower classes are more strongly associated with physical labour, sexuality and food production, or, in other words, things to do with the body. All of these things involve the lower senses of taste (production and consumption), touch (sexuality and work) and smell (both bodies and spaces). It does not seem strange, then, that there has been such a strong emphasis for philosophers on vision, as it is the sense that distances us most not only from the body, but from the physical work, pleasure and care that bodies need in order to be sustained.

Taste is a radically different kind of sense from all of the others: our tongues and taste preferences vary, and taste happens not just on the tongue but in the interactions between the tongue and the food we eat. Much of the work on taste has also been in the abstract. That is, we think about the way we 'taste' but not the way that we taste chocolate, coffee or cheese. Much has been written about tasting wine, but wine is the quintessential example of an extremely complex flavour profile that many people do not have the experience or the vocabulary to understand. Some might suggest that it is not the job of the philosopher to examine particular foods or particular taste experiences; rather it is that of the gastronome, historian or anthropologist – or perhaps the food journalist or restaurant reviewer. But I am convinced that the most interesting philosophical problems come from real-life examples. This book focuses on the problems that real-life tasting and eating produce. I hope I can persuade the reader that there is much previously unacknowledged philosophical interest to be found in this area.

1

Good Taste and Bad Taste

It's hard to make sense of the word 'taste'. Part of the difficulty lies in the fact that its literal meaning (gustatory taste) and its metaphorical meaning (taste as preferences) tend to be used interchangeably. Sometimes, it is not even clear which is which. It does not help that one can also have good taste (preferences) in gustatory taste. Most people who talk about having *taste* are focused on what it means to have *good taste*. Presumably, having bad taste is not merely the lack of good taste. Is bad taste just being attracted to, or having preferences for, the wrong kinds of things? Is it a lack of knowledge of design, structure or flavour? Or is it really a reflection of poor moral character? Historically, bad taste has been understood to be all of these things, but today it is not considered to be so closely tied to morality, just a way of dismissing people whose tastes differ from those of the dominant social class. If the ability to taste food and to appreciate its subtleties is used as the basis for understanding good taste, then we have a linguistic and experiential anchor for our metaphorical claims of good taste in art and culture. Understanding the relationship between gustatory taste and taste preferences is key to the enquiry in this chapter, since the concept that underlies both meanings is a kind of value judgement about how we sense things in the world around us.

Metaphors are so firmly ingrained into our language that we often hardly even know we are using them. In fact, it is hard to describe anything without using metaphorical language. 'The world is my oyster' is not about living in an oyster, or even eating oysters, but about having everything one wants. 'I'm on top of the world' might mean you have ascended a hill or a mountain, or it might just be the *feeling* of having done so. 'You have such good taste' is a compliment that has nothing to do with how well you taste food, but rather how well you decorate your house, dress yourself, or even which things you like in a shop. Understanding metaphorical expressions is one of the most difficult things about learning a new language, since metaphorical phrases often do not translate well from language to language. They tend to make little sense when translated literally. Metaphorical phrases take on their own meanings.

This is what has happened in the case of taste. Having good taste is the metaphorical description of having gustatory taste. But this particular metaphor is difficult to translate directly, since being able to detect differences in food and drink is not at all the same as having good taste in art, culture or design. It is even more confusing considering that not only has good taste (preferences) taken on its own meaning, but the language often does not even refer back to the original meaning of having to do with gustatory taste. Perhaps, however, it *is* a clear metaphor if we assume that 'good taste' is really about having a particular kind of pleasurable response resulting from a certain kind of understanding or knowledge of what you are tasting or looking at. Understanding what we mean by taste seems a necessary first step.

What exactly does it mean to taste? Ironically, the etymology of the word taste goes back to 'the senses relating to touch.'[1] This includes probing, testing and examining, and this is where we get the notion that 'a taste' is to have just a little bit of something. Although taste cannot happen without touch, it is no longer the first thing we think of when we consider any of the meanings of taste. The literal (gustatory) sense of 'taste' refers to the way the tongue perceives the flavours of food and drink. But in the aesthetic sense of 'taste' – where we are thought to have good taste or bad taste – the distance of vision is built into the notion. That is, having good aesthetic taste is the ability to reflect on, and understand cognitively, what aspects of a work of art are executed successfully and, by being able to articulate those, to then determine what is good and what is less good, and why. Aesthetic taste suggests that we can contemplate from a distance some work of art or music and make a good judgement. Only the cognitive senses (vision and hearing) allow for that sort of contemplation, whereas taste, touch and smell require direct bodily engagement in order for sensations to arrive.

The notion of taste includes a number of seemingly incongruent features. We taste flavours with the tongue; taste involves both smell and touch (and temperature); we can taste-test a small amount; and we have preferences or 'a taste for' various things, including the arts, foods or activities. Having aesthetic taste (well-developed preferences) ends up as a metaphor for gustatory taste, but it is not at all a clear parallel or mere descriptor for tasting what we eat. When we taste with the tongue, we have a direct sensory perception. When we *have* taste we have no direct perception, but we are able to make evaluative judgements about things that are in the cultural realm around us, including art, music, fashion, design or style. Gustatory taste is in the mouth; aesthetic taste is in the mind. Unfortunately this means that the metaphor is a tough one to interpret, since having good taste, in food or art, seems as though it should at least reside *either* in the senses *or* in the mind. But we talk about having good taste, or the right kinds of preferences, with both food and culture.

Accounting for Taste

The Latin phrase *de gustibus non est disputandum,* or its more common English translation, 'there is no disputing about taste', usually comes up in discussions where people can't agree and so revert to simple relativism: 'I like what I like, and you like what you like. End of discussion.' But what could be more subjective than what people like in food? It seems wrong to me to think that the only two ways of resolving such discussions are either absolutism or relativism. In fact, it does not seem possible that anyone really believes this: people regularly give reasons for thinking their favourite movie is the best, that their favourite restaurant is the best or that some particular painting is worth spending the time and effort to go and see. People spend time discussing the ways in which they are justified in thinking that their preferences are warranted. Roger Scruton argues that matters of taste are what people *most like* to argue about. For him, 'Reasons are given, relations established, the ideas of right and wrong, correct and incorrect, are bandied around with no suspicion that they might be inappropriate.'[2] We do this when we discuss films and their questionable merits, the plots of book or even our favourite sports teams. Yet there has to be some sort of meaningful position in between the extremes of relativism and absolutism, since in these discussions we regularly outline either latent or explicit criteria by which we judge. The absolutist would say that there are better and worse wines, or paintings or stories, and that there are qualities that can be specifically pointed out that make them superior. They might say that there are objectively better things. The relativist would say, I like what I like, and I cannot be wrong about what I like. For instance, I love artichokes and I dislike beetroot. No one can convince me to like beetroot. I understand that other people like beetroot, but learning more about it cannot convince me that it will taste good, and I will not be persuaded by a new way of preparing it.

The first problem with this kind of reasoning is that we are conflating the ideas of something *being good* and someone *liking* it. I can recognize that something might be good, or even brilliant, and still not like it. My disliking it does not make it bad; it might just not be my preference, or to my taste. This is a distinction between what is *in* the object, and my preferences about the object. Second, there are qualities or properties of food or art *in* them. Red wine, for instance, has the quality *red*, and that *is* in the wine. My perception of it does not change the fact that it is red. If I am colour-blind, the wine is still red. There is also something that wine *is like*, and that is different from what it is like *for me*. This is the difference between the objective and the subjective relationships we have with wine. When I taste something wonderful, I might suggest that you must try it because there is something in the food that I want you to taste, and not because I think you will have the exact same experience that I had. I hope you will have the same experience I had, but no two palates are exactly alike. Palates are trained by experience, time, culture and genetics and we do not all like food in exactly the same way. Some people like spicy foods; some cannot tolerate them. Some like cilantro (coriander) and for some it tastes like soap (this is a genetic aversion that is linked closely to its smell).[3] So another important distinction is that between properties in food and the experiences that we have individually. This same distinction works just as well with art objects such as paintings (there are properties of the work, and experiences of those properties). It is easier to say that this is less subjective, however, since two people can look at the exact same painting and have two experiences. When we eat, we cannot share the exact same bite.

In addition to these distinctions, we can pay more or less attention to our experiences, and to our taste experiences especially. Sometimes we eat quickly and do not notice the subtleties of flavour. Some people are trained to pay attention to the nuances of taste (or painting or literature). Sommeliers are trained to detect the types of grape, the chemical properties of the soil the grapes were grown in, and chemical properties of the wine which resemble the smells and tastes of other foods – blackberry, oak, cherry, pear and so on – that untrained people simply cannot detect. (A sommelier once told me that if I could not taste anything I could identify in a wine, just to say that it tastes like a baked potato.) It is not the case that those properties are not *in* the wines, but that not everyone has the training and ability to detect them. The (wine) sommelier preparation course is extensive training for taste – perhaps the most complex taste education there is. The body of knowledge covers history, theory, science, geography, geology, proper service and, of course, taste. Only the most exacting tasters can pass the tests needed to qualify as a sommelier; they can identify subtle differences between wines grown all over the world. A trained art historian will have a *different kind of experience* from the untrained person when they view the same pieces. The trained person will likely be able to derive more pleasure from various artworks. They should be able to articulate what it is about different works that is successful and less successful, as well as why they might be interesting because of their historical significance. They should be able to articulate why they like a work. The same artwork incites different experiences in two different people, just as the same bottle of wine can give two different tasters completely different experiences.

The Problem of Taste

The eighteenth century was a watershed moment for philosophical aesthetics and notions of taste. The so-called 'problem of taste' questioned whether 'beauty', and other notions of aesthetic excellence, indicates that there is some sort of quality *in* the objects we perceive, and that beautiful things would arouse some sort of aesthetic emotion, or distinct pleasure in the perceiver, for those trained to perceive it. The question came down to whether beauty was in the eye of the beholder (subjective), or if it was inherent in the object (objective), waiting for those who were capable or educated to perceive it. Beauty, unlike knowledge, was always indicated by a feeling of pleasure that would accompany it. Some called that pleasure aesthetic, to distinguish it from other kinds (such as intellectual or sexual), but it was always a pleasure that seemed to be linked to the body.

One of the first eighteenth-century influencers was the German philosopher Alexander Baumgarten, who offered up a conceptual change that ended up shaping much of the field of aesthetics. Prior to Baumgarten's work in 1750, 'aesthetics' was understood in the way that the ancients wrote about it – having to do only with the bodily senses or sensations. The ancient Greek notion of *aesthetikos* related only to sensory perception and the way we interpret external stimuli in our worlds. Baumgarten suggested that sensory taste was not all that mattered, and that good and bad cultural taste needed to be understood more completely. This had to do with the burgeoning art market that was developing in Europe, and the growing capacity to buy art as a consumer product by people in the middle class. What constituted good taste and bad taste needed to be clarified, but who decided what was good was even more important. According to Baumgarten, good taste was the ability to detect beauty in an object. He said that this ability came from trained senses rather than a trained intellect. Someone with good taste has the ability to judge perfections and imperfections through the senses.[4] As it turned out, this changed the whole field of philosophical aesthetics. All of a sudden, there was a real emphasis on whose senses were trained properly and how they became trained. And, of course, the focus ended up on the arts of vision (painting, sculpture and architecture) and hearing (music, drama and literature). Hardly any attention was given to the tastes experienced in the mouth.

After Baumgarten, David Hume and Immanuel Kant dominated the discussion of taste. Kant was intimately acquainted with Baumgarten's work (and sketched out much of his own most famous work in the book of Baumgarten's that he was reading) because of his proximity to him, but there is no evidence that Hume had seen Baumgarten's work at all. Although Hume and Kant did not come to the exact same conclusions, they did both tackle the question of whether good taste was an issue of good judgement in the bodily senses, or whether it was a purely intellectual matter. Hume advocated a way of thinking about aesthetic judgement that indicated that beauty was *in* a work of art or literature (his examples were mostly taken from literature). Experts, or true judges, as he called them, were able to discern, dig out or clearly identify cases of beauty much more reliably than someone with an untrained eye. He said that it was clear that 'whoever would assert an equality of genius and elegance between Ogilby and Milton . . . would be thought to defend no less an extravagance, than if he had maintained . . . a pond as extensive as the ocean.'[5] Almost everyone knows who John Milton is. But who is John Ogilby? Well, he was a much lesser-known Scottish cartographer of Hume's day – presumably some sort of hack, compared to Milton. There is discernible genius in Milton's work that will be detectable indefinitely, but a few hundred years later, no one will know Ogilby since his work really contains no genius, no beauty and nothing with any real staying power. Only true judges or 'ideal critics' will be able to identify these works reliably, since they have had plenty of practice in making comparisons and should always be able to explain why something is good or bad. True judges have good taste, according to Hume. Those with bad taste might *prefer* Ogilby, or, in current trends, a 'Velvet Elvis' painting, Stephanie Meyer's *Twilight* series or paintings by Thomas Kinkade (the so-called 'Painter of Light'). These works have all been identified as lacking in real quality and skill, despite their popularity. Presumably, no one will be learning about them in art history or literature classes in a hundred years.

What about the example of wine? Ironically, even though most of Hume's examples throughout his essay are about literature, he does use one very important parable about wine to make his point crystal clear. Hume recounts a story from *Don Quixote*:

It is with good reason, says Sancho to the squire with the great nose, that I pretend to have a judgment in wine: this is a quality hereditary in our family. Two of my kinsmen were once called to give their opinion of a hogshead, which was supposed to be excellent, being old and of a good vintage. One of them tastes it; considers it; and after mature reflection pronounces the wine to be good, were it not for a small taste of leather, which he perceived in it. The other, after using the same precautions, gives also his verdict in favor of the wine; but with the reserve of a taste of iron, which he could easily distinguish. You cannot imagine how much they were both ridiculed for their judgment. But who laughed in the end? On emptying the hogshead, there was found at the bottom, an old key with a leathern thong tied to it.[6]

For Hume, the fact that the two tasters described different tastes in the wine demonstrates clearly that flavour and taste (he mentions sweet and bitter specifically) are not in the mind alone, but are some of the qualities that we perceive in objects. A true judge would have been able to identify both the leather *and* the iron because of what Hume called a delicacy of imagination. Those who are not trained (the training, according to Hume, includes experience, comparisons and this delicacy of imagination) would not necessarily have bad taste *per se*, but they would not have good taste either. Bad taste would be more about being oblivious to any sort of standards rather than not being able to detect them correctly.

Hume is what we call an objectivist. He thought that the objective reality of beauty was *in* objects, waiting for us to comprehend it. With the right kind of training and education, one could identify it if it were present in the object. Immanuel Kant, on the other hand, was a subjectivist of sorts. He thought that the subjective character of aesthetic judgement was the basis of good taste. He argued that any one of us could make valid aesthetic judgements that were dependent upon a few very specific conditions. The most important of these conditions is that we must be able to make a disinterested assessment, or that we can separate ourselves from financial, emotional or personal interest in the thing judged. The judgement must also be both *universal* and *necessary*: we would assume that everyone (universally) would agree with the assessment that a work is beautiful, and that there are good reasons for it to be true (necessarily). Lastly, a work must be used or appreciated for its intended purpose and not judged mistakenly as something it is not (paintings should be judged as paintings, not makeshift tables). Kant distinguished between a *judgement* and that which was merely *agreeable*. In practice, this is the difference between saying 'this is beautiful' (a judgement) and 'I like this' (it is agreeable to me). Saying something is beautiful is a universal claim, because this statement assumes that everyone would agree.

For Kant, only those objects perceived through vision and hearing were considered beautiful, since they are the only ones that we can contemplate at a distance, or disinterestedly. There is no possible way to assess or judge a taste that is in one's mouth without thinking about swallowing it and taking it into one's physical body. The things we eat and drink can be said to be agreeable, but they cannot be beautiful, according to Kant. This is because something in your mouth, as much pleasure as it might bring you, and as wonderful as you think it might be, cannot have universal appeal – it cannot be considered good to everyone because it is in only one person's mouth. It is a particular experience that cannot be replicated in the way that looking at a painting might be. Furthermore, for Kant, the beautiful is something that is necessarily small and comprehensible, as opposed to something sublime, huge or incomprehensible (such as a hurricane or a mountain range). So the beautiful is small, understandable, bounded and contemplated from a distance (such as paintings in a museum with nice frames around them). That which is in your mouth can only provide a direct sensation that cannot be contemplated. But you might like (or dislike) that which is in your mouth.

Without going too far into Humean and Kantian aesthetics, we can take a few things from this lesson. Hume claims that beauty (flavour, perhaps) is *in* a work that we contemplate. Kant says it is in the *mind* or mental capacities of a well-trained person who is appreciating the work. Hume says that well-trained experts can detect real beauty if it is *in* the object. For Kant, people who are equipped with the right mental capacities are the only ones fit to judge. Kant says that only things that can be contemplated disinterestedly can be beautiful, and this automatically disqualifies food and drink. Hume agrees. So how is it that we have developed this metaphor for having good taste in culture when, according to these two, it is seemingly impossible to have good taste in food and drink? Something has to go: either one cannot have good taste in food and drink, or Hume or Kant might both be wrong. Far be it from me to accuse the giants of philosophical history of being wrong; I can say only that we no longer think about good and bad taste in that way. They were searching for a very specific kind of beauty and were trying to work out whether beauty was in an object or in the mind. Either way, the prevailing question was: *who was fit to judge* art to be beautiful? Whoever was fit to judge was deemed to have good taste.

Earlier I said that there should be some sort of middle ground between the objectivist and subjectivist attitudes. It seems now that if we take a bit from both Hume and Kant, we can acknowledge that there are properties in objects (like sweetness or bitterness) *and* there are properties in us that come only when we experience art or food objects. It does not have to be one way or the other. Since we do not all have the same capacities for experiencing (we have different training, and exposures in particular), we are not all going to have the same experience when we eat the same food or look at the same painting. Those experiences are not the same as our preferences. Hume gave us some terminology for that, as well. He said that we can have a thousand different 'sentiments'

– or opinions, or preferences – but there is only one judgement, which is understood to be a statement of fact. Sentiments and judgements are very different kinds of claims and it is important not to confuse them.

The Morality of Taste

These accounts are the standard ones usually given in philosophical aesthetics about taste, but as with so much of philosophy, these accounts are often presented without historical context or influences. According to Alex Aronson, at the beginning of the eighteenth century the social values of 'true' wit, politeness and taste underlay the upcoming philosophy of the period.[7] What that meant for these theories of taste was that they reflected a time where people were beginning to talk very openly and very pedantically about social class distinctions and what we might now call middle-class morality. The middle classes were starting to notice that the taste of the aristocracy seemed to be declining, especially when it came to morality. This was first evidenced in the theatre, of all places. It was observed not only that the characters in plays were becoming more degenerate, but that the members of the audience were beginning to behave like the characters on stage. Aronson notes that the so-called taste of the high class 'was lacking in seriousness and high moral qualities.'[8] What was considered good taste was being imitated by the middle classes, but it was not coming off all that well. It was the upper classes that ended up not looking good, because they were both behaving badly and choosing aesthetic experiences (wine, paintings, music and fashion) not because they were inherently *good* but because they were *fashionable*. In other words, what people with taste chose was popular, rather than necessarily good, and that was why people liked it. One journalist wrote in 1738 that 'taste is not that fashionable *word* of the fashionable *world*, everything must be done with taste – that is settled; but where and when that taste is, is not so certain . . . I have only been able negatively to discover, that they do not mean their own natural taste; but on the contrary that they have sacrificed it to an imaginary one of which they can give no account.'[9] Good taste became 'imaginary', because it really just seemed arbitrary. It became a form of snobbery. Proper manners, decent meals and the enjoyment of complex and important works of literature were all becoming too hard to make sense of. The moral uprightness that ought to accompany the proper and difficult work that should come with social class and education was falling into merely admiring what was popular. People could not specify what was good about fine things; they just wanted to emulate what others seemed to be liking.

An important aspect of this philosophical history which is typically left out of standard accounts of the aesthetics of taste is the relationship that both Kant and Hume (among others) had to the burgeoning moral theory of the day. Hume and Kant are known more for their ethical theories than for their aesthetics, but the two theories are not unconnected. Part of the fabric of the Enlightenment, within which these philosophers were working, was a moving away from religious explanations, religious governments and the idea that emotions were a central part of moral development. Emotions were to be considered irrational and not to be trusted. But early in the eighteenth century, Adam Smith dominated the field of what we now call moral sentiment theory. This kind of account argued that what we needed to be moral was not pure reason and logic, but the things that made us human (and not robots), such as compassion and empathy. Smith argued that the best moral theories grow from the foundational assumption that we are social beings who care for one another. Accounts that suggested pure rationality would not give voice to the ways in which we really prioritize caring for our loved ones. Robert Solomon points out that, during this time, 'in popular literature, the advent of the "women's novel" inspired a literary flood of widely read pot-boilers and romances which equated virtue and goodness with gushing sentiment.'[10] Early in the eighteenth century, sentimentalism and compassion (believed to be womanly emotions) were seen as virtues in the arts, but this quickly came to an end with the advent of the Enlightenment thinking that focused on reason and individualism. By the end of the century, Enlightenment rationalism had taken over, and sentimental and emotional values were dismissed as being shallow and anti-intellectual (particularly since they were associated with women). Good art was supposed to be challenging and interesting. It left room for diverse interpretations, but it was not emotional or trivial. People with good taste liked good art; those who liked bad art had bad taste.

This link between bad taste and the emotions has not disappeared, even now. By the end of the eighteenth century, sentimental novels and romances were dismissed by the enlightened in favour of more rational works. Jane Austen, who was best known for her sentimental novels about women and their desire for meaning in their lives outside marriage, had been largely put aside in favour of more masculine authors and characters who tackled man's engagement with nature. These included Herman Melville's *Moby-Dick* and the harsh realities of growing up and city life in Charles Dickens's *Hard Times*. This was the beginning of a shift away from valuing sentimental art as good and towards shunning it because it was too emotional. Others have said that sentimental art, or kitsch, is not bad because it is emotional but because it is too easy. Sentimental art does not challenge us; it is just pretty and nice. There is nothing to interpret and no ambiguity. But really, this is just a clear cultural preference for the intellectual over the emotional that was established with the moral theories of the day.

Sentimentality eventually came to be perceived as a moral defect. When Kant wrote about morality, it was to be understood as completely and essentially rational. Our capacity for reason is the essence of what it is to be human, and his argument was based on the fact that we cannot make moral decisions without full understanding. Being moral is about the ability to apply universal rules to particular situations, and to be able to articulate why you have made the moral choice you have. For Kant, 'melting compassion' was to be done away with completely in his absolutist ethics.[11] Universal rules applied (rationally) to all people equally. This was the end of emotion and sentiment, and of the moral sentimentalists. This form of rationalism was never really dug out of ethics after Kant until the twentieth-century 'care ethicists'. For an important part of our history, one that I am afraid really has lasted, emotionally driven actions are considered less rational and thus less moral. The more disinterested a choice is, the better it is, because it is more rational.

I provide this background not because I think they were right, but because these arguments of the eighteenth century have made their way into the common vernacular of today. To some extent, good taste and good morals *are* associated with reason, complexity and formal (and aesthetic) education. These characteristics also tend to be associated with men. Bad taste and bad morals are associated with emotion, simplicity and a lack of education. These characteristics tend to be associated with women. Although these might be sweeping generalizations, there is much evidence throughout history of this belief in the association between women and emotion, and we have taken up many of the eighteenth-century arguments for reason to dictate our directives about government, freedom and our legal system. What we have inherited from the eighteenth century is a notion of good taste that needs an 'ideal observer' – one who is distanced, rational, reflective and able to understand a work of art within a particular historical and artistic context. Emotion is generally considered a weakness and something that interferes with the proper reflective distance required for one to consider a work rationally.

To sum up, we have seen how so-called good taste comes with the right kind of training, a proper distance so as to contemplate it properly, and the right kind of attendant emotions. It all leads to what the twentieth-century sociologist Pierre Bourdieu suggests: taste is construed not as a matter of proper training, but of sheer socio-economic class distinctions that lead to particular kinds of desires and tastes. As it turns out, 'proper training' is directly connected to socio-economic class. He argues that having good taste is connected to understanding culture, in the true anthropological sense of the notion of culture. Cultural taste has to do with preferences for cultural objects like art and design, but anthropological taste only happens when we consider that 'taste for the most refined objects is reconnected with the elementary taste for the flavors of food.'[12] Historically, only the wealthy classes had access to a wide variety of food, or food from different cultures, or what Bourdieu calls cultural capital. Typically, the wealthy classes eat less because they are allowed to be more focused on form than on function. This is how the wealthy can sustain themselves on micro-greens, foams and dishes that are the size of small flowers – because the *form* they come in is where the skill is displayed. According to Bourdieu, working-class people expect objects to perform particular functions while the upper classes are allowed a more distanced stance (or gaze) that is more detached from everyday life. Culinarily speaking, the poor typically eat a larger quantity of lower-quality foods that come in a smaller variety. This can be seen easily in the twenty-first century with the wide dispersal of eating-related illnesses (especially obesity) in the lower classes, although it is certainly not limited to the lower classes. The lower socio-economic classes buy the foods that are the most filling for the their money. That is, foods that are high in calories and often not as nutritionally beneficial.

What Bourdieu ultimately argues is that taste – the ability to really differentiate between the qualities of different flavours – is the capacity to develop preferences for some flavours over others. But without exposure to many different foods and flavours, one would never be able to learn to differentiate. He considers this to be a form of code reading, something akin to understanding a language, but that is limited to the ways in which culture functions. For those who cannot 'read' that code, it is not that they do not *see* the symbols, but that they just do not *understand* them.

To understand Bourdieu better, it is helpful to begin in the Middle Ages. According to Massimo Montanari, a historian of food, there was no understanding that some people had a more 'refined' sense for the taste of food than others. People believed that 'the same legitimacy of all tastes [was] determined by the natural instinct of each individual.'[13] This was partly grounded in a religious belief that in God's eyes, all people are equal. In the early sixteenth century, Count Giulio Landi wrote in praise of his Piacentino cheese (a Sicilian goat's-milk cheese coloured with saffron and studded with whole black peppercorns), 'However much the populace may recognize its goodness, not for that can they provide the reason why it is so good.'[14] In other words, commoners might like the cheese but not be able to say why. So some might like the cheese, others might be able to say that it is good and say why, and still others might be able to say why it is good and properly appreciate the superiority of Piacentino cheese. If one could say why it is good but still be just as happy with an inferior cheese (think processed cheese slices, or spray cheese), their ability to taste well, to have good taste, should be called into question. So it is here that the first real differentiations were made between classes where taste becomes 'a mechanism of social differentiation', which arises from 'the need of the elite to reaffirm at all times their difference, attributing it to a "rational consciousness" which they do not recognize in the peasantry'.[15] The upper classes had access to higher-quality foods, and were regularly taught to appreciate them in ways that the lower classes never were. This social division has been important in a number of different areas, but probably nowhere more so than in their ability to enjoy fine wine.

Wine is an easy example with which to understand this concept, since there are many people who have not been given the training and experience to detect the incredibly subtle differences between wines. Theoretically, anyone could be trained to detect these differences and to develop preferences for the most coveted flavours and flavour combinations, but access is realistically restricted to those who can afford a wide variety of wines. For Bourdieu, having good taste is about the ability to read a cultural code, and the code of taste has historically been limited to the upper classes through access and privilege. The metaphor extends even further from food and wine to the cultural sphere, where access to museums, concerts and literature are part of the fabric of the expectations of the elite. Having good taste, according to Bourdieu, is merely being trained to like the things that the elite like. There is no ideal observer for Bourdieu, except that some are more enculturated than others into understanding the culturally significant signs of their culture.

Bad Taste

If good taste is about liking, preferring or finding pleasure in the right things, then bad taste must be about liking, preferring or finding pleasure in bad art, bad food or even things that are immoral. People with bad taste find pleasure in the *wrong* things. Only a few people have written specifically about what constitutes bad taste, compared to the hundreds who have written about good taste. Apparently the standards by which we judge taste to be bad are considered less important than those we apply to what is good, or we just assume that bad taste is what those who do not have good taste have. Robert Solomon makes it clear that bad taste is not just about liking bad art. Bad art (see the Museum of Bad Art for some great examples) just demonstrates 'sheer technological incompetence'.[16] Solomon argues that although some people have bad taste because they have not been trained to understand a medium or what might be in fashion in a given culture, it can also be the case that people like things that are morally bad. We might say that those who have bad taste are attracted to 'the forbidden, the blasphemous, the vulgar expression of the inexpressible, the provocation of the improper and cruelty (for example a bar stool whose legs are actual stuffed Buffalo legs).[17] While I do not think that having bad taste in food or drink is often about liking immoral things, it might be about either liking standardized things, or not having any awareness of your own preferences.

Taste is not just direct sensation on the tongue. All taste involves some cognitive awareness of what it is that we are tasting, and whether or not it is good. I can recognize a strawberry that has gone bad and also recognize it *as* a strawberry. I recognize good strawberries as well, but some cognitive reflection is still required to be able to tell the difference between a strawberry and an orange. I might also have a preference for strawberries over oranges, but that does not require any knowledge *per se*. I agree with Ted Gracyk when he says, 'Good taste is developed by learning consciously to make the discriminations necessary to specify what aspects make an object aesthetically good or bad, where one's enjoyment is grounded in the process of identifying the good and bad features of one's preferences.'[18] Thus *preferences* do not require knowledge, but *taste* does. Bad taste is having strong preferences without the reason or justification that would be required to differentiate between possibilities, and is therefore a form of wilful ignorance. Unlike bad or wrong-headed thinking, however, where one might guess at an answer without being able to reasonably deduce or explain why it is correct, with taste, and aesthetic preferences more generally, the attendant aesthetic pleasure is an essential part of that choice. Aesthetic preferences include honed aesthetic pleasures as well as a cognitive part that can help to focus those pleasures.

Ted Gracyk also outlines a set of conditions by which bad taste might be constituted. He says that someone (X) would have bad taste if all four of the following conditions hold:

(i) there are connoisseurs for the specific tradition in question;

(ii) X systematically prefers works other than those admired by the connoisseurs, even when directed to those features which connoisseurs find most rewarding;

(iii) the works preferred by X are preferred on the basis of personal experience of them; and

(iv) X has appropriate education about that tradition to understand what connoisseurs look for and value in that tradition.[19]

Ultimately there have to be established cultural standards that X is aware of and has experience of, but X still prefers other examples. No one *likes* the art in the Museum of Bad Art; it is just that they have such classic examples of failed technique that it is hard not to chuckle at it. But people *do like* Thomas Kinkade paintings, for instance. These paintings are immensely popular. Kinkade, the self-proclaimed 'Painter of Light', created a whole industry around paintings that evoked a sense of longing for nature, comfort and warm light that primarily comes from cosy fireplaces and candles. One commentator claimed that the popularity of his art 'tells us something about his public, about a desperate yearning for nostalgia that pervades parts of American life, a return to the safe glow of some imagined past'.[20] It is this idyllic imagined past – one that Kinkade took up some years after Norman Rockwell – that critics seem to dislike the most. Kinkade himself led a life that was difficult in ways typical for a painter (alcoholism and some seriously bad behaviour), but he also had huge monetary success in his lifetime, which was not typical for an artist. Kinkade's paintings are not controversial or challenging; they are of lighthouses, cottages and houses with ambient light emanating from inside the windows. The houses are set in nature and exude serenity and peace. As one commentator says, 'It's mainstream art, not art you have to look at to try to understand, or have an art degree to know whether it's good or not'.[21] At his height, Kinkade had stores in 350 malls all over America.[22] His paintings, however, are kitsch. Eventually he started including Disney, DC Comics and *Star Wars* characters in his paintings, to bring home the kitsch ever more strongly (just imagine *Lady and the Tramp* in a peaceful landscape setting). His paintings started to feature on La-Z-Boy recliners, and a whole line of mugs, pillows and blankets. Kinkade's paintings are plentiful (they are not all painted by him, especially now that he is dead) and cheap (relatively speaking for artworks). His art appeals to the masses because it is easy to understand and very sentimental. It is the kind of thing many people would want to hang in their homes. Kinkade's website claims that his works are displayed in over 10 million homes in the U.S., and that 'he is the most-collected living artist of his time.'[23]

So do people who like Kinkade paintings have bad taste? According to Gracyk's guidelines, it depends on whether or not one has an education in what is valued in twentieth- and twenty-first-century painting. Those who are unaware of standards, who might be drawn to paintings that are sentimental in the way Kinkade's are, would be excused from criticism that their taste is bad since they just did not know better. An art critic who loves Kinkade would be shamed, however, since the paintings, though displaying some technical skill, are not interesting or challenging in the way that the 'fine art' of this time aspires to be. Having good taste, then, depends on the individual, not the things to which they are attracted.

The culinary analogy to Kinkade paintings is processed food. The principle behind processed food is reductionism. That is, various foods are taken apart, reduced into their basic component parts and put back together in a way that guarantees absolute consistency. In that process, additives can be put in: vitamin D might be added to milk, or vitamins to white bread that replace those lost in the process of bleaching the flour. Pop Tarts, for example, use bleached, standardized flour, so that every Pop Tart tastes exactly the same, all the world over. The same goes for Easy Cheese, Oreos and much breakfast cereal. The flavours of these foods are manipulated so that each tastes the same in every single package. No effort goes into tasting variations of any of them, in the way that one might pay attention to what apples are used in a homemade pie, or what combination of spices might be in your banana bread. All the effort goes into making sure that it tastes the same every single time. The taste variation is the thing that forces tasters to pay attention to differences, and to recognize which flavours they like and which ones they do not. Without the subtle variation, palates never have the opportunity to recognize and reflect. I love Oreos, and I love that they taste exactly the same every time I eat them, but I also know that my love of Oreos comes within the context of a number of other foods that I eat that help me to recognize the flavours that Oreos provide.

The Taste of Wine

Wine is one of the most complex substances that we regularly taste and ingest. More people drink it than really understand its complexities, but as with all foods, we consume it for a wide variety of reasons, ranging from wanting to be intoxicated, to enjoying a glass with dinner, to tasting its complexities or just practising identifying them. If I drink to get drunk I am not paying attention to the possible complexities that my glass contains, but neither am I doing anything wrong. Sometimes we eat merely because we are hungry, not paying attention to each bite, but this does not diminish the ways in which we can eat to taste. It is no different to walking past a painting when you are in a hurry. The question arises as to who has good taste in wine and who has bad taste.

Surely there is no clear litmus test. But as has been shown in this chapter, there are a few good guidelines. Certainly there is a large set of connoisseurs of wine, and the criteria of those connoisseurs are very clear.

Wine is considered the consummate indicator of people who have good taste. It is perhaps the most complex beverage on the planet: the multitude of factors that can change its flavour are so immense that it must be controlled and understood by a work-force with incredibly refined palates. Winemakers use techniques (and some vines) that have been around for hundreds of years, and they strive each year to maintain the quality, consistency and flavour that they are known for. Wine culture has well-developed systems of training and certifying, ensuring that people are able to taste discerningly and consistently. Galileo Galilei once said, 'Wine is sunlight held together by water.'[24] It is our ability to *ingest* that liquid sunshine, not just to taste it, that gives us a truly existential experience like no other. Wine is the ultimate expression of place, and to be able to ingest different places is one of the premier experiences of eating and drinking. When we taste the different places of the world, not only do we get to enjoy the wide variety of flavours but we are at once connected to each place, to the land and to the people who made the wine. With wine, to taste is not just an ability to *identify* correctly, but to really *appreciate* what one is tasting. In order to appreciate, one must understand how to taste, and what goes into winemaking that makes it such a special drink. Wine's ubiquity is not coincidental with the fact that it is alcohol, which both warms and excites. Really appreciating the taste is something that one cannot do without exposure to a wide variety of wines from all over the world.

There are a number of ways in which to determine who has bad taste in wine: people who buy the wine college students buy, people who buy very cheap wine, people who buy wine from the supermarket bottom shelf and people who buy almost any White Zinfandel (but especially Sutter Home, who invented it). All of these wines tend to be sweet and not very complex. They are made in big batches with low-quality grapes that are completely standardized so that the flavour never varies from year to year or bottle to bottle. White Zinfandel is considered a 'beginner wine' because it is sweet and simple, and people tend not to continue to drink it after they have understood some of the pleasures of more complex wines (although to be fair, there are some really excellent White Zinfandels).

While it is still questionable as to whether food can be art, it can at times be something that we can interpret and ascribe meaning to. It is at least unquestionably aesthetic. Simple foods, like processed cheese, do not change and are not complex. Wine is at the opposite end of that spectrum – it varies from grape to grape and winery to winery. Sometimes a bottle spoils, as we can tell from the smell and certainly from the taste. Wine tastes different the longer it is open. People who love wine often love to talk about wine as they hone their own wine vocabulary, and also try to work out whether they are tasting the same things in the wine as the people they are with. In describing wine we can ascertain if we are having the same kind of experience as others.

Gustatory taste is only part of what it means to have good taste in wine. Given that we know that there are properties in wine available for tasting, as well as variations in us that are dependent on age, experience and genetics, good taste is really about proper appreciation. The properties of wine are neither good nor bad, but we develop knowledge of all kinds about the properties that we value in the wines we prefer. Appreciation is about accurate identification in conjunction with the ability to identify the properties in a wine that one likes. Good taste is not about knowing which wines are supposed to be good and ordering those to impress others, but about really being able to identify which characteristics are pleasing. This cannot be done without a great deal of education, not just about different flavours but about why certain wines have the flavour profiles they do, and what part of the geography, landscape or climate might have had an impact on a certain vintage.

Wine culture, in some ways like art culture, has many internal celebrations and competitions. Each year, several competitions for the 'best wines' are held all over the world. Until the mid-1970s French wines had always been considered the best. Culturally, they were considered superior because they were the seat of the Old World, where wine had been perfected and had its longest history. In 1976, however, a California Chardonnay from Chateau Montelena (Napa Valley) was declared the winner of the 'Judgment of Paris' wine competition. Steven Spurrier, a British wine connoisseur living in Paris, had put the competition together in order to introduce France to some of the newer American wines. The tasting was blind, but the judges preferred the California Chardonnay to the French ones. Spurrier and other connoisseurs were astonished that a New World wine could win this competition. Part of the French snobbery comes from the entrenchment of the Old World and New World divide, which they take very seriously. Old World wines claim to be the best since they have perfected their techniques over a much longer period, their vines are the oldest and the culture around wine primarily in France, but throughout much of Europe, is thought to be more refined than the wine culture of America. New World vines are literally imported to the New Worlds from the Old, but even with the same vines, the soil, geography and climate are different. The families that tend them are different, the facilities are different and the chemistry is different. All these factors produce different tastes in the resulting wines.

So how can one wine be the best? Criteria generally concentrate around the following: appearance, aroma and bouquet, taste, aftertaste or finish.[25] Usually each category is scored and awarded separately, with an additional judging category for overall impression. Wine competitions now abound, and if the French were astonished when a California wine won for best overall wine, they were even more dumbfounded when a wine from China won the prestigious Decanter World Wine Award. Steven Spurrier, the same connoisseur who set up the Judgment of Paris in 1976, established the Decanter competition in 2004, hoping to raise the level of French wines even more. In 2019 Chinese wineries took home seven gold medals for their wines in the Decanter competition, including in the categories of red, white and rosé.[26] China has an abundance of arable land on which to grow vines and they have quickly acquired a taste for very good wines. Although the fact that the Chinese can produce excellent wine is not really that surprising, old ideas about French and European superiority still reign in many parts of the world (especially in Europe).

To taste food and wine well, to have good taste, one must be able to have experience tasting a variety of foods from a variety of sources. I reject the idea that taste should be construed as an objective form of knowledge. Without reflection or self-knowing, one's preferences default to the familiar. If you do not stretch your range of experience then you have only your default preferences. By stretching and experiencing new things, one expands the variety of experiences. As with the epistemology of knowing, as we learn new things, we are able to make better and more refined distinctions.

To make a judgement that someone has good taste you are required to believe that the person can not only make fine distinctions, but really feels the right kinds of pleasure when they taste. 'Foodie' is a relatively new colloquial term for someone generally interested in food, tasting, gourmandism and food preparation. Foodies tend to take particular delight in eating, well beyond the interest in food that people have to satisfy their hunger. In contrast, a 'foodist' advocates a certain kind of diet, such as vegetarianism or veganism. There is no possibility that a purely objective taster will exist. Perhaps there might be chemical analysis, but part of the built-in subjectivity of being human is to do with the fact that we have only subjective experience on which to depend. This built-in subjectivity does not stop us from recognizing that some tasters are better, and more qualified, than others. Professional wine tasters, coffee tasters and so on are used the world over to determine quality and consistency as well as to judge whether certain foods and beverages are up to a standard of quality. But when it comes to taste, objectivity should not be an ideal. Universality should not be an ideal. As Julian Baggini explains, the 'goal should not be to separate out the cognitive from the biological, the objective view from the subjective, but to integrate them, bringing our minds as well as our mouths to our appreciation of food.'[27] It is tremendously important to make clear our standards before we judge, since having the wrong ideal might make us value the wrong things.

Baggini also points out that the Italian Slow Food movement got a lot of things right when they advocated the ideal that eating should be about pleasure, not mere sustenance. Slow Food advocates for food that is good, clean and fair. It is food that is grown well, by farmers and workers who know the land, know the crops and are paid a fair wage. Food should be cooked with love, care and tradition. Food should be shared with others: it is not meant for us to ingest alone, in the way we put fuel in a car. Eating together is a special act, perhaps even a sacred one, and thinking about where food comes from, how it was prepared and who cooked it should not be peripheral to the real delight we have in it. There are a lot of 'shoulds' in what I just said, and I am admittedly making claims about what I take to be an ideal situation. I believe that having good taste involves having a relationship with food that goes well beyond what happens on the tip of the tongue. We develop tastes for things that we think are good, and right, and what we have been exposed to. Having good taste takes a conscious effort.

2

The Pleasures of Eating
and Tasting

Pleasure is slippery. Is it physical or mental? Good or bad? Can we have too much? Some people associate pleasure with happiness, but then question what exactly the relationship is between them. Some associate pleasure with the body, but since the body works against the mind, they wonder how best to subvert or control pleasure. Others understand pleasure only in reference to its opposite, pain. Some try to define pleasure, or to capture its essence, which has proven to be a relatively fruitless task. Others connect pleasure to aesthetic experience, but have never really worked out whether or how pleasure is necessary or sufficient for aesthetic experiences to happen, even though they seem clearly connected. Others still want to give an account of pleasures in their higher and lower forms, with quantitative values assigned to different kinds of pleasure.

We begin here with more questions than answers: is pleasure a state of the body or the mind? Is it necessary for happiness? Can we have a theory of pleasure that is not dependent on pain, ethics, aesthetics or accounting? Although I do not think I can really address any of these specific questions in full, I do want to *defend* pleasure. I think it is good, and I think it is human to pursue it. Eating provides a great model with which to understand pleasure. Taking pleasure from food is something that everyone, everywhere, can do. What kind of pleasure do we get from eating (savouring, not just 'feeding')? And can pleasure be considered something that I can develop an account of as good, human, significant or even essential?

A Bit of History

Pleasure, especially the pleasure derived from eating, has been seen as dangerous or subversive from our earliest philosophical days. This seems to be because of its connection to the body and its upending of reason. Socrates noted the tight connection between pleasure and pain as he had his handcuffs removed just before being put to death.[1] He remarked how closely connected pleasure and pain are as he rubbed his hands together and pleasure flowed in where the pain was. He says that pleasure and pain 'will never come to a man both at once, but if you pursue one of them and catch it, you are nearly always compelled to have the other as well; they are like two bodies attached to the same head.'[2] Socrates suggests that had Aesop thought about it, he would have made up a fable about pleasure and pain engaged in constant quibbling, their heads fastened together; where one of them went the other would be forced to go as well. Plato also talks of pleasure and pain as being opposite states of the soul, with a neutral state between them that is a sort of calmness. He suggests that this neutral state is often mistaken for pleasure when it follows an experience of being in pain. Socrates sees pleasure, calm and pain as being on a continuum that is objective, but being at one extreme of the continuum makes people think that being in the middle seems more like experiencing the other extreme. There is an objective scale moving from painful to pleasurable, but it is always a subjective experience that varies from person to person. Socrates' only reference to food and pleasure is to describe hunger and thirst as painful states. He says that satisfying hunger by eating is pleasant, and 'drinking is a satisfaction of the deficiency and a pleasure.'[3] Eating and drinking are only pleasurable in that they alleviate the pain of a deficient state of the body. So he sets up a dualism of pleasure and pain as being natural states of the soul, but he never really says what pleasure is, and he does not talk about eating as being pleasurable except as it alleviates hunger.

For Aristotle, pleasure merely *completes* an activity but is neither good nor bad in itself. He also says that pleasure 'belongs to the province of the political philosopher; for he is the architect of the end, with a view to which we call one thing bad and another good without qualification.'[4] He thought everything had an end or a goal towards which it was directed. The goal of acorns is to be oak trees; humans aim to be happy. Aristotle thought pleasure was just a by-product of both individual and collective hard work, but should not in itself be the goal that humans focus on. If we reach our goal, then we experience pleasure. If we can identify what it is that we want, then we can begin to build good habits so that we can start doing that which will get us to our goals. If I pursue higher education, for instance, I will derive pleasure from the steps that I complete on my way to achieving that goal. This seems OK so far. But Aristotle says specifically that pleasure itself cannot be a goal, for if it was then we might achieve that end by merely being high on drugs, in a food coma or constantly pursuing sexual gratification. Ultimately, these are not the things that make us truly fulfilled. He also says that many pleasures are not in fact good but are base and offensive, and that some pleasures are actually harmful.[5] Pleasure, for Aristotle, is not a goal but a process that accompanies other kinds of goals. Pleasure is only a by-product of the pursuit of happiness.

The separation between pleasure and activity for Aristotle seems to go back to the ability to find a mean between extremes of diet. This is not just finding the right amount to eat, but the right kinds and balance of food, which are determined by age, activity level, culture and access, among other things. The right diet for an athlete is different to the right diet for a sedentary person. The right diet for a child is different to the right diet for an older person. The best diet would have to include pleasure in eating, too. But, as Aristotle recognized, there seems always to be *akrasia*, or a 'weakness of will'. Given the opportunity, many people will choose foods that do not allow for this perfect balance. This weakness of will is what accounts for the times we indulge in something we have told ourselves we would not have. For me, this weakness is usually around chocolate.

St Augustine, in the fourth century AD, wrote extensively about how sexual desire was worrying for him, as was the desire for food. Augustine was key in reviving Christianity in the fourth century, but he also wrote about original sin, the Church being like a 'City of God' as opposed to an earthly city, and the role of grace in Christianity. He wanted to argue for a world where religion could help its citizens to be good; it would help them make better decisions for themselves and their communities. As it turns out, eating and sex are also central topics in his writings. Both eating and sex have proper goals according to Augustine: health and reproduction respectively. But one can overindulge either of these when one derives pleasure from the *excess* and not just for the primary end. He says, 'and while we eat and drink for the sake of health, there is a dangerous kind of pleasure which follows in attendance with health and very often tries to put itself first, so that what I say that I am doing, and mean to do, for the sake of my health is actually done for the sake of pleasure.'[6] There is a proper goal (health) and an indulgent goal (gluttony). Each offers a different kind of pleasure, but it looks the same from the outside – eating. There is nothing wrong with taking pleasure in eating, but it causes concern when one tries to separate the pleasure from the good (health) when one has no interest in the good. The same rules apply to sex. Sexual pleasure for reproduction is fine, but if one indulges in sex merely for pleasure (say, with contraception) then you have moved from the good (or goal) of an activity to the pleasure alone. This, he says, is when we get ourselves into trouble. Sexual pleasure is fine in attendance with reproduction. It is *supposed* to make reproduction more pleasurable. Eating is great in attendance with health. Beyond that is the pleasure–danger zone. These proper goals help to keep the pleasure we associate with eating and sex in check, but it seems that there are so many exceptions when it comes to these pleasures that it can be hard to make sense of. For instance, if one cannot have children for a variety of reasons (age, medical problems and so on), or one does not *want* to have children, then one should not have sex at all, according to Augustine. IVF (in vitro fertilization) would be out of the question, since this is reproduction without sexual pleasure. Given that homosexual sex cannot result in procreation, that seems to be out of the question as well. As for eating, how do we know how much to eat before we have gone off the edge? One Oreo? Five Oreos? Ten Oreos? Health seems to be an ambiguous goal, since it does not seem to correlate directly with how much we eat. For me at least, pleasure is not always about how much I eat, but how much I enjoy what I eat.

Augustine's account also says that the pleasures we find in eating come only from alleviating our hunger, filling the belly. But what about the pleasures we get from *tasting* good food? The goal of tasting is not health. The goal of tasting is pleasure. Practically, it might be about identifying foods that are poisonous (as poisonous foods tend to taste very bitter), or detecting sweetness, which often indicates fruit that is at its peak ripeness. But tasting good food is something that goes well beyond just the practical. Eating can be considered practical, but tasting can also be pure pleasure. Given that tasting involves taste, smell (which brings in memory) and touch (temperature as well as texture), eating is really a multisensory activity that has the potential to generate intense pleasure. Eating slowly, savouring and choosing your favourite foods are all ways not just to stimulate the tongue, but to produce genuine gustatory pleasure.

Jeremy Bentham started from a completely different place to Augustine. He wanted to come up with an account of ethics, or obligation, which appealed to no religious principles. He argued for a system of both happiness and fairness that was grounded in explanations of pleasure and pain. According to Bentham, pleasure and pain are our most basic motivators and so any explanation for why we do or do not do certain things would have to start there. He begins his utilitarian theory by explaining:

> nature has placed mankind under the governance of two sovereign masters, *pain* and *pleasure*. It is for them alone to point out what we *ought* to do, as well as to determine what we *shall* do. On the one hand the standard of right and wrong, on the other the chain of causes and effects, are fastened to their throne. They govern us in all we do, in all we say, in all we think: every effort we can make to throw off our subjection, will serve but to demonstrate and confirm it. In words a man may pretend to abjure their empire: but in reality he will remain subject to it all the while. The *principle of utility* recognizes this subjection, and assumes it for the foundation of that system, the object

of which is to rear the fabric of felicity by the hands of reason and of law.[7]

This principle of utility begins and ends with pleasure and pain. Note also that it is 'nature' and not God who puts us in this situation. The only good is pleasure, and the only evil is pain. No original sin here. Since, according to Bentham, one's life is an aggregate of pleasures and pains, one must do all that is possible to make the pleasure outweigh the pain. Otherwise, life is dominated by pain and suffering, which is the worst kind of life for human beings.

In this passage two different kinds of hedonism are outlined: psychological and ethical. Psychological hedonism is the position that all *motives* are for the perceived good of pleasure. That is, all of my choices are made because I believe that I will feel pleasure as a result. I drink coffee in the morning because of the rush of caffeine that I find pleasurable. I exercise because I believe I will feel the pleasant effects of warming my body, the exhilaration I feel while I do it, and the satisfaction of it being done. Ethical hedonism, on the other hand, says that the pursuit of pleasure is the *best* and *highest good*, and that actions are right or good only insofar as they produce pleasure and avoid pain. Ethical hedonism then makes a moral theory out of finding pleasure in doing the right thing. So if pleasure is the goal (and pleasure is a universally human goal), the pursuit of pleasure will always be good. Since Bentham's account was about accumulating the most possible pleasures, he sorted them out according to intensity, duration, certainty or uncertainty, and propinquity (proximity) or remoteness. He added two additional categories: 'fecundity, or, the chance it has of being followed by sensations of the *same* kind, and purity, or, the chance it has of *not* being followed by sensations of the *opposite* kind'.[8] The more pleasures one has, the better the life one has. Although this sounds slightly, well, hedonistic, it does seem to be what many people actually believe.

John Stuart Mill, a great friend of Jeremy Bentham, added to Bentham's account that intellectual pleasures should be counted as significantly more desirable than the lower pleasures. He said that there might be different *qualities* of pleasures, which changed the kind of account that Bentham advocated, where the goal was to try and amass as much pleasure as possible while at the same time diminishing the amount of pain one suffered. Further, consistent with Enlightenment thinking, no one person's pleasure counted more than any other person's, and this so-called 'hedonic calculus' or 'pleasure calculus' was an attempt to come up with a rational and scientific method of measuring pleasure, and therefore measuring good. For Mill, pleasure is the good. It is the primary goal for humans. But for him, intellectual pleasure was *more good* than physical pleasure. Goodness and virtue are then directly associated with the mind and intellectual pleasures – learning, reading and understanding – but not the bodily pleasures. The body is only capable of the lower pleasures. Eating, being of the body, cannot be virtuous.

Mill's principle of utility says that 'actions are right in proportion as they tend to promote happiness, wrong as they tend to produce the reverse of happiness. By happiness is intended pleasure, and the absence of pain; by unhappiness, pain, and the privation of pleasure'.[9] Pleasure and the absence of pain are, according to Mill, the only things that are good in themselves. Mill also spelled this out in what have become infamous comparisons. He said that it is so obvious that some pleasures are better than others that choosing lower pleasures over higher ones would be like choosing to be an animal over being human.

But the way he put it is pretty stark. He noted that 'it is better to be a human being dissatisfied than a pig satisfied; better to be Socrates dissatisfied than a fool satisfied.'[10] This is his argument (or perhaps a mere metaphor) that there should be a sharp distinction between higher and lower pleasures – that no one would choose to be an animal or a fool and to give up their higher pleasures. Higher pleasures are, of course, pleasures that are intellectual, produced by vision and hearing, but also pleasures that come from contemplation, understanding, and higher-level knowledge. As a postgraduate I had to study ancient Greek. I was sure that it would never make any sense to me. I knew I was good at memorizing things, so I imagined that I would just memorize my way through two years of Greek with likely no understanding. But while I had to do my share of memorizing, I came to really understand the language, and I could read it without much effort (eventually, after a *lot* of memorizing). I probably had some similar feeling about conquering geometry at school, but that memory is much fainter. Those are intellectual pleasures – working hard to understand, getting to the end of a long novel, finishing a class you are interested in and have worked hard for. This feeling of satisfaction is what Mill means when he talks about the higher pleasures. Lower pleasures are corporeal. Touch, taste and smell are all dependent upon the body and on close proximity to an object. He says that anyone who would choose lower pleasures over higher ones does so only because they do not know the higher pleasures. Higher pleasures are longer lasting, he says, and are seemingly inexhaustible. Mill also says:

A cultivated mind – I do not mean that of a philosopher, but any mind to which the fountains of knowledge have

been opened, and which has been taught, in any tolerable
degree, to exercise its faculties – finds sources of
inexhaustible interest in all that surrounds it; in
the objects of nature, the achievements of art, the
imaginations of poetry, the incidents of history, the
ways of mankind past and present, and their prospects
in the future.[11]

Or, in other words, smart people can find anything to occupy
themselves. Some pleasures are more desirable than others, some
are more intense than others, but the better the pleasure, the
more *good* it can bring. For Mill, then, pleasure is a good, and
intellectual pleasures are higher goods than the lower pleasures.
There is a problem, though: when the body is tied to the lowest
part of us, and maybe even to vice or viciousness, we begin to
see the mind as good and the body as bad.

So far, Mill's theory makes some intuitive sense. Mill has set
us up with a dichotomy that no one can deny. Would I rather be
a pig or a human? Well, a human, of course. But do I sometimes
indulge in the so-called lower pleasures over higher pleasures?
Yes, we all do. This extreme dichotomy forces a theoretical im-
possibility, since in real life we do indulge in bodily pleasures
sometimes. I eat biscuits at night, and sometimes even ice cream.
Those are bodily pleasures, and it does not make me an animal
if I decide to eat ice cream instead of reading philosophy before
bed. The obvious evidence for this is that academics, and people
who live a life of the mind, are a vast minority of the population.
This is further evidenced by the fact that so much of the population is overweight, has excessive drug and alcohol addiction
problems, and sex addiction is on the rise. Many people still
smoke, even though we all know it is not good for us, presumably

for the short-term buzz (and it works as an appetite suppressant). Most people do things that are physically pleasurable over finding intellectual pleasures, even those who *know* full well the power of the higher pleasures. But we are still human. Many people even choose to die sooner than necessary (either knowingly or unknowingly) rather than change their diet by giving up meat, fat, sweets and so on because they like the way they taste and like the way certain foods make them feel. Many people refuse to be vegan or vegetarian, even though excessive meat consumption does damage to their bodies. One of the most common reasons people give when faced with the realities of factory farming and the environmental harms that intensive animal farming cause is that 'it tastes good.' It has been shown clearly that humans do not need meat, and we certainly do not need as much as we eat, but we like meat so much that we are willing to live with the cognitive dissonance (or just dismiss that out of hand) that meat-eating causes. Eating meat, for many, provides so much pleasure that any pain endured is worth it. But this does not make us animals or fools. Inasmuch as we balance the pleasures we pursue, we eat things we like, we study things we find interesting and we fill our time with the things, people and foods we find the most pleasurable.

Meat-eating and night-time ice cream, physical comfort found through touch, sex, drinking alcohol and even lying on the sofa watching TV are all physical, or bodily, pleasures. We cannot do without them. But Mill's point is that we need to seek the intellectual pleasures to gain *real* happiness; we cannot live our fullest life *only* seeking pleasure for the body. Being human means we need mental stimulation too.

Part of the problem I see with this kind of accounting is in making a strict distinction between physical and intellectual pleasures, as I do not think that there is a clear line between the two. Pain, however, seems a little easier to pinpoint. If I drop something on my toe, I feel an intense pain in that toe. I do not have to search to find the exact location of my pain. If I have a headache, I at least know that the pain is in my head and not in my hand, even if the pain is a little less focused. If I have the flu, my pain seems to be all over, but it is still very physical. But if I am suffering from grief, or worrying about my finances, these kinds of pain are not really locatable in my body. They are existential pains, maybe even intellectual pains. They are judgements of understanding, assessment of loss, but they are psychic, not bodily, although the effects of these might be felt in the body too. If I am depressed, I can become physically drained for no apparent reason, and I might change what I would normally do, like stop exercising, which will have an impact on my body. So the physical pain might be locatable more easily than the mental, but it is not clear that they are not deeply intertwined.

Feelings of pleasure are not easy to pinpoint. I could be touched lovingly or have my back scratched, and the site of the pleasure is very specific, but most pleasures, even physical pleasures, are not. I like to exercise because I like the way it feels to push hard, work up a sweat, feel my heartbeat rise, and I feel better for the rest of the day. I like to eat things I enjoy, not just because of the way they feel in my mouth, or because of their taste, but because of their effect. I like the way sugar, caffeine and alcohol make me *feel*, not just the way they taste or because they make me less hungry.

Physical pain tends to be much more precise in the body than pleasure. Pleasure and pain are really only contraries in a limited sense. Physical pleasure is more amorphous than pain is. So when we see pleasure and pain as being equally located in the body, it actually gives pleasure a more physical accounting than it really has. Because we are so embodied and our bodies and minds are so co-mingled, we do ourselves a disservice by claiming that we know things about what happens as if they are separate. We also do ourselves a disservice if we think that pleasure and pain are felt in the body in the same way. What follows from this is another mistaken notion that physical pain and intellectual pain are fundamentally analogous to physical pleasure and intellectual pleasure, and that if we could make a quantitative assessment tool, then we could calculate the best ways to maximize pleasure and minimize pain. But it seems to me that human happiness (never mind human goodness) does not work that simply.

What all this history has taught us is that pleasure is incredibly difficult to pin down, but that it seems to be an essential part of human experience that needs to be accounted for somehow. Do we count it? Diminish it? Treat it as a side issue or just own up to it and admit that we just love pleasure and it is part of being human? If we own up to it, we can flip the model that relies exclusively on vision to produce knowledge and the mind as being self-determining over the body. If we start with taste and pleasure, then we make both the tongue and the body central. Because, if you think about it, eating and snuggling are not merely physical. They have an impact on the mind as well, as we feed it (literally) and nurture it through human connection.

Eating also literally connects us to the world around us because we *consume* it. It connects us to other people because we do not produce and prepare all our food ourselves. Eating fills our bellies, but it also gives us pleasure – satisfaction at cooking something good, reminders of childhood favourites, and detecting a superior quality in a dish or ingredient. Tasting also gives us *knowledge* of what it is we are eating – what possible ingredients were used and how well a dish was executed. The pleasure from tasting comes from savouring flavours and textures. And this is really just a matter of paying attention. It requires one to slow down, savour and really concentrate on what is going on inside one's mouth. Pleasure from this kind of appreciation is completely different from alleviating hunger, except that the two activities, eating and tasting, are inextricably linked.

Pleasure: Physical, Mental and Emotional

The notion of pleasure is often generalized to what we mean when we are feeling good, and we understand it most often in the way that we understand its opposite, pain. Pain can be much more specific and localized, but pleasure sneaks in as pain diminishes, as well as when we are feeling emotionally, spiritually or even physically delighted. However, the notion of pleasure does not make a lot of sense beyond actual examples. The concept of pleasure is so broad that it bridges the gap between the mental, emotional and physical. I can feel pleasure thinking about a loved one, downhill skiing, or eating chocolate. What could these possibly have in common? In addition, we also experience visual pleasures, auditory pleasures and the pleasures of smell, taste and touch. It hardly seems possible to account for the wide variety of experiences that we all experience as pleasurable, not to mention that what *I* find pleasurable others might not, so there is a radically subjective element as well. I understand that other people find pleasure in eating beetroot while I most definitely do not. It seems as if the different experiences of pleasure might be as broad as human experience itself.

Another difficulty in making sense of pleasure is that many pleasures are experienced in very bodily ways. That is, sensory pleasures are experienced through the body before they can be processed mentally, remembered or expressed verbally. Interestingly we also tend to use the term *sensory* pleasure, rather than *bodily* pleasure, but pleasure tends to be much more closely associated with the bodily senses, touch and taste, than the pleasures associated with vision and hearing. It seems easier to account for things in terms of ideas, concepts, mental attitudes and beliefs, and oughts. Pleasures do not fall neatly into these categories, but neither do they fall neatly outside them.

For Roger Scruton, there is a clear distinction between intellectual and sensual pleasures. He says that intellectual 'pleasure is not immediate in the manner of the pleasures of the senses, but is dependent upon, and affected by, processes of thought'.[12] He says that when we hear poetry read, it is not the hearing of the words that gives us pleasure, nor the sounds of the music when we listen to a symphony, but the *meaning* that we ascribe to those sensations that allows us understanding. We can derive intellectual pleasure from art, but it is from the meaning and interpretation, not from the raw sensory input. Sensory pleasure, on the other hand, is *unmediated* by thought on this account. We just feel it, or sense it. Touch, for example, does not need to be interpreted: we just feel it and like it. Sexual pleasure is more sensory (or more bodily) than listening to music or contemplating a painting, and here again we distinguish pleasure by both the character of its object and its proximity to the body. Scruton says that there is always some thought that goes into experiencing pleasure, but that one can still make a meaningful distinction between intellectual and sensory pleasures. This dichotomy itself, however, worries me. It implies that 'intellectual' and 'sensory' represent two realms that characterize very different kinds of experience, and that they might be mutually exclusive. He goes on to explain that the distinction is really clarified by both internal and external connections to thought. Sensuous pleasure, he says, has only an external, accidental connection to thought, while intellectual pleasures have an intrinsic or internal connection. I might find pleasure in eating a nice meal, but it will be enhanced by understanding the preparation of the food, or the origin of the ingredients. For Scruton, the eating is merely sensory, but thinking about the origin, or gaining knowledge of the cooking techniques, might be where the pleasure really lies. This does not seem right to me. Perhaps there are both intellectual and sensory pleasures, but I do not think it is possible to reduce this to intellectual pleasures alone, or to minimize the significance of the sensory so much as to take it out of consideration.

The philosopher Barbara Savedoff also thought this distinction was cause for concern. She writes about Scruton's division that it has 'no teeth', and that all pleasure, even sensual pleasure, requires thought. She claims that there is no such thing as pure sensation unmediated by thought.[13] Daniel Dennett might differentiate between these as 'raw and cooked feels' (or sensations). But, unlike data, feels or sensations are always at least a little bit 'cooked'. Savedoff gives the example of the ways in which 'our pleasure in a work of art requires not only that we recognize it as art rather than nature, but also that we recognize it as the particular type of art that it is. Our enjoyment of a painting depends on our not mistaking it for a *view*, but also not mistaking it for a *photograph*.'[14] She says that this applies to other sorts of sensory delight as well. A chocolate mousse needs to be recognized as a mousse, and not a pudding, say, in order to be fully enjoyed or appreciated. We need to recognize a pear, she says, as a pear and not an apple, since part of our pleasure comes from the object of sensuous experience being an exemplary instance of that category.

Savedoff explains that 'pleasure in food is as dependent upon the recognition of the food as the pleasure in a painting is dependent on the recognition of the painting.'[15] I would add that not only are there no sensory pleasures that are not mediated by mind, but there are no pure intellectual pleasures that are not instigated by the senses. Our bodies, senses, minds and even desires can only be thought of in isolation. Nowhere do they actually exist in isolation from one another. So where *kinds* of pleasures might vary, they cannot be categorized into sensory and intellectual, or bodily and mental. These dichotomies are derivative of a well-ingrained history of philosophizing about the mind and the body, the philosopher's tendency being to diminish anything relating to the body, and to venerate the mental.

Food Puritanism

Throughout history, governments and various religions have felt the need to regulate, control and minimize our enjoyment of pleasure, especially where food, alcohol and sex are concerned. Why have they seen the need to do this? To begin with, it is not clear where the line is between experiencing pleasure and experiencing too much pleasure. Too much physical pleasure can result in drunkenness, gluttony, addiction, loss of reason or control or any other sort of behaviour that would deem a person unfit for civil society. Not all of the senses can be overindulged. One cannot overindulge in looking at a painting or listening to a symphony (although it seems clear that there can be too much pornography or violence, which are also visual). Overindulgence tends to be with touch – both sex and eating. But it is not just about the physical act of sexual intercourse or eating food. It is about the need for more and more, beyond what is healthy.

The Catholic Church has taught that the repression of desire is virtuous because desire should only be for God. Excessive desire for food, sex, alcohol or money indicates that one is not focused on the pleasure that God alone can provide. Adam and Eve partook of the fruit of the tree in the middle of the Garden of Eden (often referred to as an apple, but not explicitly named as such), which they were forbidden by God to eat (Genesis 3:1–13). Not only did this make them self-conscious and self-aware about their bodies, but in the Christian tradition, the apple, or more generically the forbidden fruit, became symbolic of knowledge, temptation, sin and the entire fall of man. Adam and Eve were permitted to eat any of the fruit in the garden, but not the fruit from the tree in the centre. They consumed what was forbidden, but not out of necessity. There was plenty of other fruit available. Excess is what goes beyond what is natural, or normal, on to the superfluous. This is what Adam and Eve were guilty of in eating that fruit – too much. It seems impossible to determine what the line is between enough and too much, but in this case it was painfully clear. They did not need it, but they ate it anyway. It is too bad that this had to happen with using eating as an example. Eating has thus become the consummate example of overindulgence, but in most cases the line is not as clear as it was for Adam and Eve. One has to teach oneself carefully the difference between pleasure and indulgence. How much food is too much? It is often hard to know.

Pleasure that is confined to eating for health leaves out too much that is absolutely human – sharing, cooking, family, celebrating, community and comfort. Eating connects us to other people in a way that is deeply profound, given the amount of work that generally goes into growing and harvesting, and preparing meals. Eating together as a family helps to build and maintain connections, and of course eating together is the basis of much business as well as courtship. Restricting eating to health (and sex to procreation) is incredibly short-sighted, given that the range of possible experiences available to us through the act of eating is immense, and helps us to interact meaningfully with the physical world around us and the people in our community.

Isak Dinesen's short story 'Babette's Feast' (1958) was made into an iconic foodie film by Gabriel Axel. In this story a particularly strict sect of Lutheranism sets the background for control over the pleasure of food – and everything else. Dinesen uses a deeply ascetic community as an example of the suppression of pleasure as a form of religious piety. Babette is a French refugee in the mid-nineteenth century who ends up in a remote town in Norway. She has been sent there by a friend who knew two sisters who lived there, Martine and Philippa, named after Martin Luther and a friend of his, Philip Melanchthon. They live a very pious life, restraining themselves from extravagances of all kinds. Babette is taught how to cook for them, a simple fare of split cod, and bread and ale soup. The sisters 'explained to her that they were poor and that to them luxurious fare was sinful. Their own food must be as plain as possible.'[16] Food, clothes, smells and sights are all drab. Babette washes the windows of their cottage to let the light in, something that none of the other townspeople would dare do, and the sisters are astonished. For Martine and Philippa, simplicity is not only a way of life, but a virtue and pride. The kind of pious life they lead represents the honour that they want to give their (deceased) father, who had ministered lovingly to both them and to the whole town.

Babette lives with them for fifteen years, and comes into some money that she wins in the French lottery. She asks the sisters if she can spend the money on a dinner, to celebrate the one-hundredth anniversary of their father's birth. Babette puts on a real French feast, involving tastes, textures, creatures and drink that no one in the town has ever experienced. The sisters and their guests have vowed not to talk of the food but only of the weather. One of the dinner guests says in advance of the meal, acknowledging how hard it might be to control his tongue, that the tongue 'is an unruly evil, full of deadly poison'.[17] He says to the guests in preparation of the dinner that we shall 'cleanse our tongues of all taste and purify them of all delight or disgust of the senses, keeping and preserving them for the higher things of praise and thanksgiving'.[18] Given that our tongues not only taste, but also speak, the dinner guests are intent on continuing to deny the pleasures that come with this meal; they would rather advocate their asceticism. They have decided collectively to experience no pleasure in Babette's food.

But they are blindsided. The food is delicious – better than anything they have tasted before. The drink is intoxicating, and allows for laughter, forgiveness, and joy. The different courses lead the guests to connect, reminisce and even rekindle some romance. The food, and the meal, are transformative, making the guests rethink what is possible in their own lives through taste, skilful cooking and camaraderie around meals. In the end, 'it was, they realized, when man has not only altogether forgotten but has firmly renounced all ideas of food and drink that he eats and drinks in the right spirit'.[19] This group is elevated by the food. It serves as a catalyst for connection that has not previously been possible with the drab fare they are used to and have insisted on. Babette teaches the group how to heighten their senses without losing their faith.

The reason this film has become so iconic among foodies is because it shows so clearly (and painfully) how the ascetic life sometimes misses the mark. Piety is not about being drab, but about focusing on the right kind of things. Babette brings into focus the ways in which the everyday can be delighted in, by bringing her artist's skill to even the dullest ingredients. And she does this not only in the special-occasion dinner, but from day to day. She gives a gift to the sisters by cooking for them something that they had never been able to imagine themselves. The dinner is not indulgent: it is thoughtful, skilful and perhaps even a work of art. Babette gives the best of herself to the sisters through food.

Why would we need the Church to moderate for us? Or a government, for that matter, or anyone but ourselves? Every few years the United States government issues guidelines for a 'food pyramid' (now a whole plate) on food groups to eat, or not to eat. Unfortunately, it changes dramatically depending on current trends in nutrition science (and the powers of various food lobbyists – especially the beef and milk industries). The health insurance industry created the Body Mass Index (BMI) so we could work out a healthy weight for our height.[20] But these are really only modern responses to what has been an age-old problem: regulating human pleasure. For as long as there have been religions and governments, this is something that has had to be addressed. Plato set us up to think that the appetitive part of the soul needed to be managed by the rational part.[21] Aristotle followed by advocating that there are both rational and irrational aspects of the soul, but that the body is still governed by the rational soul. But the early Christians, whose thought reigned much longer than that of the ancients, viewed pleasure as corporeal, and something to be controlled by a form of discipline. In this case, pleasure was often associated with the pleasures of eating. Many cloisters of monks across Europe throughout the Middle Ages ate only very limited quantities of often very plain food. There are also stories of priests who performed self-flagellation so as to punish the body, but self-denial, and especially the denial of the most pleasurable of human activities – eating and sex – was carefully regulated by the early Church.

For women, the denial of food was much more prevalent than it was for men. Anorexia, or 'holy anorexia' as Rudolph Bell writes, was a relatively common practice for female saints in the early Middle Ages. St Catherine of Siena and St Clare of Assisi were both well known for their ability to go without food as a form of self-denial, and everyone could see the visible effects in their emaciated bodies. Going without pleasure (in this case of eating) was evidence of their dedication to God. As Bell writes, 'to be the servant of God is to be the servant of no man. To obliterate every human feeling of pain, fatigue, sexual desire, and hunger is to be master of oneself.'[22] Depriving oneself of food is still seen as a virtue by many women. Seen not as dedication to God, but as a form of control over the body, millions of women (primarily upper- to middle-class white women, but not exclusively) deprive themselves daily of the pleasures of eating and the satisfaction of a full belly. Today thinness is a sign of a woman who is able to resist the regular temptations put in front of her; the more she resists, the more virtuous she is considered to be. To be overweight is to give in to these temptations, and to be less virtuous. But virtue should not be read into the body like this. Virtue (and vice) are a state of the soul and habits of behaviour. Resisting biscuits does not make one a good person. Taking pleasure in a moderate number of sweets might actually make for a better life than denying all pleasures.

I am regularly praised by my peers in the university dining hall when I get a big salad for lunch, often with 'you are so good' or 'you are so virtuous' (in fact, I am just thrilled that I do not have to cut up that many vegetables myself). And every time I see someone with a dessert after lunch they make an excuse or a justification about why they are allowed to have it, usually that they went to the gym or that they are going to the gym and that there will be some sort of *quid pro quo* of exercise for the calories they are about to consume. Sometimes it seems as though they intend to impose pain on themselves as a punishment for the pleasure they are about to enjoy. The frequency with which we have adopted the language around food being good, bad, sinful, virtuous or evil is astonishing. This moralizing of eating creates a social imposition around it that one is not supposed to *enjoy* what one eats, that one must *punish* oneself (with exercise or starvation) for eating, and that one level of virtue or viciousness has to do with the aspect of restraint one shows around food. This does not allow one to develop a healthy relationship with food. Balance is, of course, important, but if a culture imposes unhealthy moralizing about food it will be virtually impossible for children to grow up with a healthy attitude towards cooking and eating. It becomes hard to think well about food. This is what has happened in the U.S., at least, with a whole generation of parents who have drastically minimized cooking skills, a radical separation from their food's origins, an overabundance of processed, pre-packaged and fast food, and longer hours at work, meaning that they cannot invest time and effort in cooking with their families. In the U.S. the number of overweight and obese people is at an all-time high, as are eating disorders where people are starving themselves, or bingeing and purging. How is it that we can at the same time be so overweight and so malnourished? It is the effect of our culturally disordered eating.

Along with the moralizing that we do with food, we have a good bit of guilt. Speaking of 'guilty pleasures' indicates the value judgement that there are some pleasures that we just need to feel bad about. Generally, guilty pleasures are pleasures that we experience about foods or entertainment that we recognize to have little value nutritionally or that are not generally held in high regard. They are pleasures that one would feel ashamed of if many people knew about them. But just the fact that we have the common notion of guilt associated with pleasure means that we end up feeling guilty about many of the pleasures we have. Guilt is a moral feeling that one is doing or having something that one should not have. Ice cream seems to be one of the most popular guilty pleasures. It has little nutritional value and is high in fat and sugar, but it can taste really good. According to the International Dairy Foods Association, Americans eat on average 23 lb (10.4 kg) of ice cream a year.[23] Clearly, we find this food pleasurable, but is it really necessary to associate guilt or a moral failing with it as well? Presumably, as long as it is not doing us physical harm, we do not need to feel bad about enjoying it, but we have this long-standing association with feeling bad about things that make us feel good. If we associate salad with virtue and ice cream with vice, then we associate the pleasures of the body, and eating in particular, with moral praiseworthiness and blameworthiness. Pleasure will never win this battle, but it is a battle that I do not believe needs to be fought. We should delight in food not merely because it alleviates hunger, but because we have been provided with a bounty of choices, textures, combinations and cultures to taste from. Food nourishes not only our bodies but our minds and imaginations, and we can learn about the world through eating in ways that we cannot through other means. Finding pleasure in eating is not something that we should shy away from or shun, but something to be cultivated and honoured as something uniquely human.

Bodies, Animals and Health

This split between the body and the mind is one that we talk about, but it is not entirely clear that they are separate in the ways that we talk about them as being separate. We cannot just be minds, we cannot just be abstractions and we cannot just be solipsistic consciousnesses. We are minds and bodies simultaneously. We move around the world in bodies; we are in physical relationships and proximity with other people; we drink, sleep, grow, defecate, move and die. We give birth! And for me, at least, giving birth is the most profound thing that I have ever done: I grew another person (two at once, actually) inside me until those bodies could survive on their own. And those tiny bodies I grew have continued to grow and have turned into independent entities who are now as big as I am. We are *embodied*. That is, our bodies (or brains) contain our minds, and so any thoughts that the mind has are expressed *through* the body. We express ideas through writing, spoken language, and physical gestures. When our brains want us to do something, it 'tells' the body to do it – to move in a certain way, or to say a certain thing. Our minds are really not capable of expressing anything without our bodies.

We are, as a species, as physically embodied as we are mentally capable. But for some reason, we tend to talk about these attributes as though they are distinct. A full account of pleasure might be one of the first reasons to give a unified account of experience. Pleasure is not *just* touch, or *just* taste, or *merely* physical. It is *assessment* of a given situation that an experience is pleasurable. And there is a feedback loop that allows me to recognize that I want an experience to continue. I love feeling my husband's hand on the small of my back when we are out – a small gesture that he and I are connected while among other people. But the same physical gesture by a stranger would not be pleasant at all. It would be uncomfortable. It is not *merely* the assessment in either case that makes the experience either pleasurable or unpleasant, but the touch and the assessment together. Furthermore, we generally have a desire that can be filled that produces pleasure. I desire to eat chocolate, or to feel the rush of sugar that goes from my tongue to my throat to my brain. I desire to feel the touch of my husband's hand. When desires are fulfilled, pleasures evolve. I can desire food if I am hungry, but the mere filling of one's stomach seems different to me than the real, positive sensation of pleasure and the desires that are filled.

One of the things that it means to be human is to have both a body and a mind. But bodies have not always been considered trustworthy. Bodies, with which we have sex and eat, some say, are fickle and unreliable. Bodies are not stable. They need constant attention, food, sleep; they get hurt easily, suffer pain, grow and shrink. Minds, on the other hand, are constant. They are susceptible to reason, belief and judgement. This is the way much of history has approached the mind–body split, but it really is not that simple, and the approach short-changes the physical nature of our embodied experiences. Historically, bodies have been more closely associated with women, while minds have been more closely associated with men. Women experience pregnancy, give birth, nurse babies, do much of the physical work in the private sphere, and have historically cooked much of the food. For these reasons, women have been considered *more embodied* than men. Men have been more closely associated with ideas, reason and argumentation. Men function in the public sphere, run the government and make the money. But this really short-changes both sexes. Women have ideas, men do lots of physical labour, women are rational, and men can cook. And we are all embodied, and we are all human. We eat together, cook together, work together and experience pleasure (often together).

Historically, eating and sex have been the quintessential examples of sensory pleasures that are intimately linked to the body. They are also the raw, physical pleasures that we cannot do without. They are the two primary reasons that we are able to continue as a species. They are the things that we have most directly in common with animals, and we refer to them as our animalistic desires. Viewing them this way, we tend to think that they cannot be controlled and are not subject to reason or justifications. Eating and sex are of the body and animalistic. But although this is an approach that many throughout history have taken, it is also fundamentally flawed. We do share eating and sex with animals but, given that we also have higher-order capacities, we also have the ability to reflect on both of these as part of what it means to live well, to be happy and to find pleasure. Most animals do not have sex purely for pleasure. They do it for procreation, and if they do experience pleasure, they are not in long-term committed relationships where they are raising families, owning homes, saving for retirement, enjoying holidays and forming bonds with their partners that allow for the kind of pleasure that humans can have. Furthermore, most animals do not overeat. They eat what is necessary in order to maintain their energy.

What is it that makes us different, special and separate from animals? Some have said it is our capacity for reason; others say it is self-reflective consciousness, or our ability to make moral decisions, our linguistic capacities and the attendant ability for abstract thought, our ability for long-range planning, or to experience regret. In all likelihood, it is all of these things and probably many more. I am not really interested in what the *one thing* that makes us different from animals is. There are obviously many things that differentiate us. But one of the most important abilities that separates us from animals has to do with the way we cook and eat. Animals don't cook their food. Animals don't season their food. Animals don't plan their meals. And although both humans and animals all have to eat to live, all humans share this one universal trait: we cook our food. This is significant because there are not very many truly universal shared characteristics that humans have across all cultures and over all time. When we cook food, we transform it fundamentally not only into something more edible or more digestible, but into something that is reflective of cultural values, local traditions and the kinds of foods that are available in the area in a given historical period. Although we all eat, we do so in an immeasurable variety of ways, using different foods and cooking styles, and with drastically different attitudes towards our food. We also have a tendency to cook the foods we like. The wealthy have access to a wider variety of foods that may be fresher, healthier and tastier than those of the poor. People in rural areas might have access to different foods than city dwellers. People all over the world have different access to different kinds of food, and consider very different things edible or delicious.

The pleasures that come from eating are not merely gluttonous, and they are not necessarily mindlessly hedonistic. Really tasting something – savouring it, even – is one of the important ways in which we truly are different from animals. Our cognitive capacity allows reflection about what we eat, whether it reminds us of something that we have tasted in the past, or we pay attention to the subtleties of the flavours or textures. Sometimes, we just pay attention to the experience in ways we do not normally. This is one of the truly universal pleasures that connects all humans. The possibility of finding pleasure in eating, no matter what the cuisine, is one of the highest capacities we have, not one of the basest. Just because we have eating in common with animals does not mean we do it the same way they do. This capacity for pleasure is what differentiates us from animals. As humans, we also have the reflective capacity to focus on what we eat, to discern different flavours and textures and to connect food experience with previous meals, flavours and memories. Allowing and training ourselves to delight and take pleasure in eating is one of the most human endeavours we can undertake.

Jean Anthelme Brillat-Savarin, one of the West's first real gastronomes, claims that 'animals feed themselves; men eat; but only wise men know the art of eating.'[24] This sums up a number of the assumptions that we have about eating. Sometimes, when we are ravenous, we just feed. We do not even taste what we are eating, since we gobble it up too fast. In the Army they call this 'feeding the machine', or compare it to putting petrol in the car. Food in this sense is *merely* fuel – as it is, perhaps, for animals. But there is another form of eating that humans can have, even though we do not always take the time to appreciate our food. And this is what Brillat-Savarin is talking about. Savouring one's food is something that anyone can do. Food does not have to be expensive or extravagant for one to take pleasure in the flavours, textures, smells, complexity or even the crunch of a dish. The pleasure that can come from eating is not just about filling one's belly, or alleviating one's hunger or thirst. This kind of pleasure can come from a number of aspects, but one of the primary ones is really just *taste*. The ultimate for Brillat-Savarin is the *art* of eating, which involves knowledge, appreciation and the ability to taste what one is served. It probably also involves cultivated manners and civility. This is not something that is available to everyone, only to those who have been raised to understand culture and etiquette, and who have access to the kinds of dinner that require many rules.

Roger Scruton suggests that this kind of dining experience is one of the highest expressions of the cultivated human. Not only do we eat together, but we demonstrate a shared set of understandings about the highest form of human interaction, which includes the way we sit, the way we speak, how we hold our utensils, how quickly we consume our food and the topics we are ready to discuss. According to Scruton, a proper dinner party is an example of the highest form of civilization, as it requires moral, social and gastronomical knowledge to be able to do it well. It should also be one of the highest pleasures for humans, since the kind of appreciation we can have for it is of a naturally complex nature.

Finding pleasure in eating is also something that can express our humanity. That is, what it means to be fully human means taking advantage of all the facets of human nature, and differentiating ourselves from animals. Eating and enjoying our food is one of those aspects. In the ancient epic of *Gilgamesh*, written four thousand years ago, Gilgamesh's friend Endiku is considered a wild man until he discovers the island with the 'bread eaters', who cultivate wheat, process it and bake it into bread. Before that, Endiku lived in the wilderness, ate grass and drank water, like the herbivorous animals. It is not until Shamhat brings him to the island that he has the opportunity to taste bread and beer. (As it turns out, he really likes the beer!) It is only when he eats cultivated and cooked food that he is considered fully human. Of course, bread, beer and the entire agricultural revolution could be said to be the reason for humanity as we know it, but at least in this story, bread is the specific turning point from nature to culture, from animal to human, and from wild to civil. Bread in particular is a sign of civilization. In order to have bread, a community must be able to grow crops, harvest grain, make flour and then bake the bread (which involves sustained heat for baking). Endiku's 'discovery' of this culture marks his understanding and subsequent acceptance of civilized culture, urban communities and the ability to include food preparation in long-term planning. According to some, the invention of agriculture changed the trajectory of human development. It certainly tied us to the land in a way that nothing else had up to that point. From a philosophical perspective, it represents a change in the foundations of the way humans connect with each other over food. Meals are planned, work is shared and community is built.

Aesthetic Health

Since we are not perfectly rational, and we tend not to always make the right choices to best accord with our health, it seems that sometimes gustatory pleasure can also be our downfall. We eat too much, and we eat things that are not good for us. We presumably do this because we enjoy them. Kevin Melchionne suggests a way in which we can understand how we might better identify the things that create the greatest pleasure, so that we can cultivate taste. He outlines a theory of what he calls 'aesthetic health', which helps to identify and speak about 'one's own aesthetic pleasures and preferences'.[25] In order to identify preferences, one has to work out the *sources* of one's pleasure. This means being open to a large variety of experiences that the world has to offer in terms of aesthetic pleasures. As understood through food, it means that one not only knows what one likes, but likes it having experienced many other things. Melchionne explains that aesthetic health can develop 'in two directions: expansion and refinement'.[26] This means intentionally seeking out 'new experiences or creating new variations on past successes.'[27] Melchionne uses the example of a gourmand who is on the lookout for new spices, flavours or produce so as to be able to try new recipes. The snob, as opposed to the aesthetically healthy person, is one who eats only what they know. Insisting on 'maintaining a hierarchy of values than exploring what the world has to offer, the snob clings to the superiority of this or that Italian wine or French cheese as if aesthetic health depended upon this judgement really being as clear as the snob assures us it is.'[28] The snob is fixated on brands for recognition, rather than being willing to try a large variety of foods so that they can identify and articulate the reasons their pleasures are experienced.

With food, pleasure can be heightened for myriad reasons – primarily culture, family, geography and exposure. If one chooses what to eat for reasons that exclude pleasure, it becomes more and more difficult to return to the actual experience of pleasure with eating. Faced with the increasingly difficult question, 'What should I eat?', many people, overwhelmed by the variety of options, and with a radically reduced ability to cook well (at least in the U.S.), decide to impose a set of rules that limit their options. Some go vegetarian, vegan or Paleo; some go gluten-free; some decide not to eat white foods; some try any of the vast array of fad diets that include excluding an entire food group, or eating only one particular food group. These diets enforce social norms around eating, more and less strict rules around one's own food rules, and some shaming of others. This is only possible when there is no strong cultural tradition that does not generally restrict choices for daily food. In the U.S., for the most part, people can eat almost any foods, from any culture, any day of the week. We are inundated with food, cultural influences and highly processed foods that can last years in the cupboard, and we are overwhelmed with choices.

This is why diets that help people restrict their choices are so appealing, since never before in history have we been faced with the plethora of cuisines, and the immense quantity of food, that we have now.

Chocolat and Chocolate

In 2000 Lasse Hallström directed what would become one of the most important 'foodie movies'. More than just a film about the magical powers of chocolate, *Chocolat* exemplifies attitudes around food as sin, pleasure as danger, and fear of the other. It is the story of a woman, Vianne, who moves to an old-fashioned French town in the winter of 1959. She is unmarried but has a daughter. The town is deeply religious, or perhaps repressed, and is heavily influenced by a strict mayor, Reynaud, and a loving but inexperienced priest. Vianne is endearing, open and generous, but she does not fit in with the townspeople as she is much too unconventional. She shows up with her illegitimate daughter, she claims to travel with the north wind and she seems to be an outright alchemist with her chocolate. She wears bright red. Vianne comes to open up a chocolate shop, but many believe she has arrived to tempt them into sinful lives of indulgence. She opens her chocolate shop just before Lent, which seems to indicate her intentions to corrupt the town. Lent, for these people, is about self-denial, keeping up appearances and strict rules about traditions and social customs.

Vianne works her magic slowly by befriending women who also seem to have some inclination towards her untraditional ways. As the men try to control the ethos of the town, it becomes clear that there are cracks in the relationships all around – abusive and neglectful marriages, judgemental conditions put on mother–daughter relationships, and strained relations between the town and the mayor. It does not seem that chocolate will help any of this, but that is exactly what happens. Vianne says to each of the curious souls who dares to come to her shop that she can guess their favourite kind of chocolate. Sometimes she gets it right, but she always uses the opportunity to engage with people and to listen to what is really going on with them. She uses chocolate as a means to connect, but also to help heal some of the broken relationships that are happening right in front of her. Armande is an older woman whose daughter has disowned her because she behaves in ways that her daughter does not deem appropriate. Josephine comes to Vianne as an abused woman who is having trouble admitting that she needs to leave her husband. Vianne ministers to both of them with love and acceptance – and chocolate. Reynaud, the mayor, does not want to admit that his wife has left him, and Vianne's acceptance is something he cannot handle; chocolate for him is merely sinful indulgence manifested in the world. Ultimately, in a frenzied attempt to destroy Vianne's chocolate shop, he ends up with a sliver of chocolate on his lip. He takes it in and begins a different kind of frenzy, eating all the chocolate he can get his hands on. He ends up in a drunken chocolate stupor in the shop window on Easter morning. Vianne immediately forgives him and helps him clean himself up and regain his dignity.

The film culminates in an Easter sermon in the church by the young priest, who admits that he did not finish his homily on time. He says:

I'm not sure what the theme of my homily today ought to be. Do I want to speak of the miracle of our Lord's divine transformation? Not really, no. I don't want to talk about

79

His divinity. I'd rather talk about His humanity. I mean, you know, how He lived his life here on Earth. His kindness. His tolerance. Listen, here is what I think: I think we can't go around measuring our goodness by what we *don't* do, by what we *deny* ourselves, what we *resist*, and who we *exclude*. I think we've got to measure goodness by what we *embrace*, what we *create*, and who we *include*.

He gets to the heart of the town in just a few lines. He provides a way of thinking about what it means to be good in a positive way rather than focusing on denial and exclusion.

This film exemplifies matters of tolerance and acceptance, but also the important metaphor of chocolate as perceived sin, form of temptation and embodiment of physical desires. Chocolate during Lent was thought to be extra sinful, but Vianne is able to show how an approach that involves loving kindness could also involve moderation and healing. Chocolate is (for most) a form of gustatory pleasure, but it is also a pleasure which some cannot control. If chocolate is temptation and can lead to sinful behaviour, then pleasure might be construed the same way. But chocolate and pleasure are part of what makes us human, built into our lives as something that can celebrate traditions, connections and our mere embodiment. Physical pleasure and gustatory pleasure should not just be aspects of our experience that we need to control or shun, but aspects that we can use to bring balance to our lives that include eating and exercise, seeing and learning. Not to allow pleasures around eating seems to miss the point of human happiness.

If we can disassociate the negative associations with the body, pleasure can be something that is experienced as an important value. We can choose what to eat with *values*, instead of with *rules*, which might inevitably get broken. We can also dissociate eating from guilt, virtue or vice. Eating should be pleasurable; it is not something that we need to punish ourselves for doing. But a number of historical influences remain on the legacy of pleasure. I hope I have defended pleasure, and in a way that allows the reader to understand how thinking positively about pleasure can help us to engage with the world in a more meaningful and positive way than some of the older models have allowed. Given the possibilities of finding pleasures in eating and tasting, I think it is clear that pleasure should not be something that we have to moderate or control. And yet we have had so many influences attempt to make us think that way, we have taken it in as a culture. The guilt that so many have over finding pleasure in their food is unnecessary, but given the right framework with which to think, one that allows for an embodied experience of moderation and the fulfilment of desire, finding pleasure in food could be considered a natural part of living well. Chocolate could be considered not the consummate sinful indulgence, but a pinnacle of gustatory pleasure, and a delight that we can share with each other in community.

3

The Taste of Slow Food

We all have ideologies that are made of an invisible set of beliefs which influence the ways we think about the world. In terms of what we eat, the underlying beliefs we have about food are different if food is scarce or plentiful, or if we are trying to lose or gain weight. If we are sick or healthy, rich or poor, young or old, we think differently about food. In most of the U.S., capitalism has infected the way we think about eating and purchasing food. Capitalism emphasizes efficiency, low costs and high volume. When it applies to food, we get something that looks a lot like McDonald's. While McDonald's is only one of many fast food restaurants, it was one of the first and most prominent to exemplify this capitalistic mode of thinking and production. It has been radically successful and its restaurants are ubiquitous. Many more fast food chains have followed in its footsteps. But one of the primary reasons McDonald's is so successful is because its ideology about the market matches up nicely with the way Americans think more generally about consumption. Capitalism tends to encourage us to think about everything in terms of commodities, and although food is something to be bought and sold, there are important human aspects to it that cannot be commodified. These aspects – taste, community and trust – are the topics for this chapter. And while it is important not to romanticize the past as providing more fresh food, prepared from scratch, we should be mindful not to go too far in the other direction and praise processed industrialized food. Slow Food offers a more balanced view between those two extremes.

At its most basic, Slow Food is the opposite of fast food, and of a fast life. It is a both an ideology and a practice. It is a grass roots movement that began in Italy in 1986, when the first McDonald's opened near the Spanish Steps in Rome. Some of the locals who cared about food and tradition were astonished at the audacity of this multinational corporation trying to bring sterilized, industrialized and standardized food into their culinary landscape. This event has become part of Slow Food's origin story, representing both an event and the beginning of an organized movement to promote a food culture and food knowledge that is at risk of being lost. The Slow Food ideology is one that recognizes tradition, locale, quality, flavour, people, agricultural practice and affordability. Slow Foodies advocate traditional methods of preparing food, traditional organic practices of cultivation and the recognition that growing, harvesting, cooking and eating are all efforts that must be made by whole communities working together. Significantly, Slow Food also defends the notion that good food should not be expensive, and that it is a human right to be able to derive pleasure from the taste of our food. Slow Food should be affordable and widely available. It may not seem intuitively possible that all of those things can coexist, but this is exactly what advocates for the Slow Food movement have done for the last few decades, in a continuous attempt to combat not globalization, but the standardization of food and the standardization of taste.

Ideologies

It is not by chance that the Slow Food movement began in Italy. Italy has only been a unified country since 1861, and even then the northern and southern parts of the country differed wildly in terms of climate, economy, language (dialects) and food. Italy still differs in all these ways now. One of the main fault lines still runs between the north and the south on what is called the great olive oil–butter divide (olive oil to the south, butter to the north). And, of course, this divide is not just to do with taste, but with what kind of cooking fat has been the most widely available in different regions and geographies. One commentator says:

> From the fifteenth century down through the nineteenth, the struggle between oil and butter was brought to life in European paintings, literature, and street dramas as the wars between carnival and Lent, with butter marching into battle in full armour at the head of an army of animal fats and dairy products, and its arch-rival, olive oil, leads up a host of herrings, cabbage, bread, and other Lenten allies.[1]

The fact that this is even a contested topic in Italy is an indication of the deep divide that food creates in the regional cultures throughout the country. There are still twenty distinct regions in Italy, all boasting radically different cuisines.

Many Italians say that there is no such thing as 'Italian' food, but only different regional cuisines which all use ingredients local to their geography. You will not find much pasta in the north (but you will find a lot more corn and potatoes), and you won't find many thick soups in the south (but you will find lots of lemons and light, thin pizza). When McDonald's decided to break into the Italian restaurant market, the citizens did what they could to organize a protest. They set up long tables outside the McDonald's, cooked pasta and served it to as many people as they could. This initial protest included many of the values that Slow Food still incorporates today: community, big welcoming dining tables, local cuisine, fresh ingredients and, of course, lots of wine. That initial protest was the seed that turned into a movement, with meetings, conferences, organized tastings, sampling sessions, a manifesto and a clear ideology that maintains that good food is not about gourmet food, but about rediscovering the tastes of regional cooking and traditions. One of the biggest concerns about the McDonaldization of Italy was the loss of demand predicted for the small osterias and trattorias, local restaurants that typically use local ingredients and traditional recipes. The Slow Food organization promotes local food and traditional cooking. It educates wherever it can: in schools, gardens, restaurants, conferences and institutes like the University of Gastronomic Sciences in Pollenzo. The satellite organizations of Slow Food that exist worldwide are encouraged to have themed dinners, celebrations of varieties of local and heirloom ingredients and educational tastings, and to participate in local food conventions. Slow Food also advocates seasonal eating, fair labour practices, the cultural knowledge that comes with decades of experience of growing and cooking food, and both affordable and fair prices. Rather than taking to the streets to protest, or to demand policy change, Slow Food attempts to change minds at the dinner table.

Around the same time as the Rome protest in the mid-1980s, the culinary world was becoming fixated on Michelin stars and the idealization of taste as being something distant, exclusive and extravagant. Slow Food was doing its best to teach as many people as possible the merits of the particularity of the variations in flavours that come with the changing of the seasons. For instance, pecorino cheese (from the Italian *pecora*, sheep) made with the milk from spring (while the sheep graze on young flowers) tastes different from the cheese made later when the sheep are eating dried grass at the end of summer. The taste variation is considered a virtue in this cheese and the fact that it changes over the course of the year is something to celebrate and anticipate. Pecorino is one of the Italian cheeses that is produced both fresh (soft) as well as aged (hard). But what matters here is that the taste changes from season to season, and this is considered a virtue of this cheese. Slow Food also, of course, recognizes that food changes drastically with the changes of the seasons. Fruit in summer is different from the root vegetables of winter, and the changes in the nature of food match well with our changing dietary needs as warmer and cooler weather come and go. Standardized food, or industrial food, never changes but rather produces stability for our taste buds that we can rely on repeatedly, every time we taste, no matter which city we are in. Industrial food is available all year round, and with the advent of food travel we have been able to ignore the changes that bring about different food in different parts of the year.

Slow Food unapologetically values a few things: local foods cooked in traditional ways that respect the land and *all* of the hands that brought the food to the table. Advocates of Slow Food believe that pleasure is a human right, and that good food (food that tastes good and that is good for the environment) should be affordable and accessible. This seems a pretty weighty claim, but the founders and the advocates of the movement are absolutely unapologetic about this right to pleasure. To be able to derive pleasure from eating is one of the things that all humans share. But many people are deprived of sufficient food, and many, though not deprived of quantity or quality, do not pay attention to the ways in which bodies experience pleasure. Some condemn the body for feeling pleasure at all and thus deny or starve the self. Advocates of the Slow Food movement do not think that we can settle for anything less than retaining and celebrating the pleasure found in eating.

The Slow Food Manifesto outlines an unqualified ideology. It asks for consideration of the land, the farmers, the cooks and the eaters. The Manifesto was approved by delegates at the first conference of the 'International Slow Food Movement for the Defense of and the Right to Pleasure' at the Opéra Comique in Paris on 9 November 1989. It claims the following:

Our century, which began and has developed under the insignia of industrial civilization, first invented the machine and then took it as its life model. We are enslaved by speed and have all succumbed to the same insidious virus: Fast Life, which disrupts our habits, pervades the privacy of our homes and forces us to eat Fast Foods. To be worthy of the name, Homo sapiens should rid themselves of speed before it reduces them to a species in danger of extinction. A firm defense of quiet material pleasure is the only way to oppose the universal folly of the Fast Life. May suitable doses of guaranteed sensual pleasure and slow, long-lasting enjoyment preserve us from the contagion of the multitude who mistake frenzy for efficiency. Our defense should begin at the table with Slow Food. Let us rediscover the flavors and savors of regional cooking and banish the degrading effects of Fast Food. In the name of productivity, Fast Life has changed our way of being and threatens our environment and our landscapes. So Slow Food is now the only truly progressive answer. That is what real culture is all about: developing taste rather than demeaning it. And what better way to set about this than an international exchange of experiences, knowledge, and projects? Slow Food guarantees a better future. Slow Food is an idea that needs plenty of qualified supporters who can help turn this (slow) motion into an international movement, with a little snail as its symbol.[2]

This manifesto asks a lot. It asks for economic shifts, lifestyle shifts and a shift in the way we both taste and value food. It asks that we reject the fast life, symbolized by consumerism and busyness. It is *not* a demand for political regulation or a ban on industrialized food. It is a call for education, a revaluation of taste and the promise that once you have good food, your sense of taste will forever be changed and will want good food more and more. Slow Food reminds us that pleasure is something we are inherently capable of as humans, and that our food is something that can provide us with that pleasure if we let it. What is more, this manifesto implicitly argues against large-scale capitalism (which allows for increased consumerism) and its inevitable hold on us. Only with the awareness that we are shifting towards buying and busyness can we push back to choose a different kind of life, one with fewer meaningless tasks, better relations with our family and community, and a renewed sense of connection with the land and our food.

Slow Food also asks that food should be 'good, clean, and fair'. Food should be tasty and healthy. It should be clean, meaning the production should not harm the environment, the growers or the consumers. And it should be fair: affordable to the consumer and providing fair wages to the producers. 'Good, Clean, and Fair' is the motto that reigns throughout Slow Food marketing and readings. Of course, it is hard to know where much of our food comes from in our industrialized world, but the Slow Foodies think it is a worthy endeavour to find food that is sourced well and tastes good, and that it is always worth asking about origins. It is easy to find standardized and industrialized food that gives the impression that it is from a family farm and not a factory, but much of that marketing (if not all) merely creates a happy illusion that the meat is not from concentrated animal feeding operations (CAFOS) or that the tomatoes were not picked by workers who were paid well below a living wage.

I teach classes about Slow Food, and every year I take students to Italy to see what this movement is all about. We stay on a farm, eat fresh-cooked meals from different ingredients grown on the farm, and go to several local artisans to learn about cheese, wine, truffles, fish, pasta and honey. We kill a lamb, dress it and cook it, so we really know where our meat comes from. The whole experience is pretty idyllic (except when we kill the lamb). But every year, when I come home to the U.S., I struggle to maintain the Slow Food diet and lifestyle. I shop at the farmer's market as much as I can, and I have taken cooking classes to learn some of the local specialities of my region, but there is so much working against me that it is a Sisyphean battle. Any progress I make is undone by the next trip to the supermarket or fast food restaurant and every takeaway we order.

This is exactly what the Slow Food movement is fighting against: the standardization of taste that comes with industrialized food that is exactly the same in every supermarket, every packaged cracker and every drive-through. And thus the tension. Large multinational food companies (think Nestlé or Starbucks, for instance) work incredibly hard to produce food that tastes exactly the same whether it is in Ohio, California or Europe. Oreos taste exactly the same wherever you buy them, as do McDonald's hamburgers. This consistency of taste provides people with some comfort, especially while travelling in a foreign food landscape, where it is at times desirable to be able to predict exactly what it is that you will be able to eat. But this desire for predictability and consistency has caused a fear of difference. This manifests itself in the economy where there is less demand for artisan producers and so thereby they produce less and less. Skills are not handed down from generation to generation, and speciality products cease to be made. Certain tastes and flavours are lost, just like species that become extinct.

Here, what becomes extinct is not a species, but a taste – a *flavour* that can be produced only with particular knowledge of food that grows in a particular climate, influenced by variations in the weather, perhaps, and made by those with knowledge of balance, seasonings and flavour. Slow Food, not incidentally, is generally very simple. No heavy sauces, no complicated recipes. The food is delicious because it starts with excellent, flavoursome ingredients. But when the ingredients become standardized, and we have access to only one variety of tomato, for instance, that tomato has been genetically developed to travel without bruising, to be the same size as its neighbour tomatoes, and to be exactly the same, consistent colour. It is not bred for taste or texture, but for its ability to travel well. If supermarket tomatoes are all we know, then the variety of flavours is lost. A tomato then merely *appears* as a tomato but does not provide the huge variation of acid, colour and texture that it might in other circumstances. If we (consumers) do not *know* that there are other varieties available, then we become accustomed to the supermarket variety and lose interest in developing a taste and curiosity about tomato possibilities. If we do not have access to heirloom tomatoes, then the knowledge of their taste evaporates.

In response to this concern about the loss of flavours and tastes, Slow Food has started what they call the 'Ark of Taste'

(*Un'Arca del Gusto per salvare il pianeta dei sapori* – an Ark of Taste to save the planet of flavours). Reminiscent of Noah's Ark, the Ark of Taste seeks to catalogue and save traditional flavours and products from the flood of standardization. The Ark is a list – incomplete, of course – that attempts to catalogue specific regional products and producers. The list is kept online and published in a newsletter. The Ark of Taste was developed in order to preserve the foods that are at risk of extinction because small-scale family farms are dwindling, consumption patterns are changing due to a more industrialized diet and, of course, climate change is occurring, which is impacting local ecologies more than we can even imagine. Given that so much of the food produced in the developed world is grown with no respect for season or biodiversity, this list is an attempt to salvage what is being produced in traditional ways, in specific climates.

In 1992 the European Union began legislation on the Protected Designation of Origin (PDO). In order for a product to be awarded PDO status, it must be shown to be made only with local ingredients and only within certain local regions. These laws certify that products labelled as originating from a particular region actually have originated there. This kind of regulation was necessary to protect the reputation of regional foods, to promote the sale of artisanal products and to protect them from unfair competition that misleads consumers. Imitations, which of course always abound, are inevitably lower quality and have inferior taste. These protections extend to wines and specific wineries, cheeses, cured meats, olives, olive oil, breads, beers, balsamic vinegar, several vegetable varieties and a great deal more.

Carlo Petrini, one of the founders of and primary authors writing about Slow Food, discusses a particular example of PDO Asiago cheese. About 1.3 million rounds of Asiago are produced each year. There is a subset of this cheese called Asiago Stravecchio (meaning very old), which is produced only from milk obtained during summer pasturing. The milk is sweet with flowers. Asiago can be aged for as little as only one month and then sold, but the best Asiago Stravecchio must be aged for at least eighteen months. Cheesemakers have come under pressure to sell their cheese early before it is fully aged, if they have the buyers. The Ark of Taste exists to encourage the production and sale of this aged cheese and to convince buyers that the flavour is worth waiting for – and paying for. Of the 1.3 million rounds of Asiago made each year, only about 10,000 are aged for long enough to make the Stravecchio. But if there is no knowledge of it and no demand for it, then there is no case for the producers to wait for it and not sell off all of the cheese earlier. The demand, says Petrini, 'must convince the herders to continue to spend their summer in their alpine huts; preserve the traditional breed of cattle, the Rendena; and age the cheese properly instead of selling it when young to the dealers.'[3] Without knowledge, without demand, this cheese would be lost to history.

Roquefort cheese also has a Protected Designation of Origin. Roquefort is a kind of blue cheese common in France, but in order to be labelled as Roquefort, the cheese must be made with the milk of a specific breed of sheep (Lacaune) and must be aged in the natural Combalou caves of Roquefort-sur-Soulzon in southern France. The moisture levels, yeast and bacteria found in those caves are geographically unique and give the Roquefort cheese a distinctive flavour that is impossible to replicate in a different environment. Some studies suggest that Roquefort has anti-inflammatory properties and can help to cure chlamydia (because of its penicillin-like mould).[4] So, health benefits aside, Roquefort cheese cannot be made in a factory, or anywhere other than in the south of France. Of course, it is one of the most popular French cheeses, and attempts to sell imitations in mass quantities to people who cannot tell the difference and make money off the forgery have long been made. In 1961 there was a French court ruling that similar cheese made with sheep's milk could be sold, but it could not be labelled Roquefort unless it was aged in the caves of Roquefort-sur-Soulzon. Specific climates, elevations, temperatures and bacteria combine to make one singular product. The taste of that product is unique.

Slow Food as a Moral Obligation

The Slow Food movement has made claims about food that it should be good, clean and fair, and its primary goal is to educate, train and gather people on how to do this well. There are hundreds of local chapters of Slow Food around the world, as well as conferences, tastings, markets, classes, book clubs and supper clubs. But it does not seem to have made a big impact on the way most people eat at home – or when out. Most people I talk to in Italy are familiar with the Slow Food movement and Carlo Petrini is a household name, but that does not seem to be the case widely outside Italy. Could the multinational food corporations have really won out on the taste front, so that we have stopped caring about taste and place? As an advocate of Slow Food, I want others to be convinced of its benefits, and not because it is more economical, or more supportive of local farmers, which are common reasons to eat Slowly. The reason I want to eat Slowly is for taste. Slow Food makes overt associations between food, taste and place. Food should not taste the same everywhere, since food is fundamentally tied to the land and the people who make it. But we are building a food system that does not hold that belief.

Rather, the giant food conglomerates encourage us to believe that food can be processed into its most basic ingredients, formed into packaged food so filled with processed sugar and preservatives that it can last a lifetime without going mouldy, and distributed globally. It is sold cheaply, one does not need skill to heat it up, and washing-up is easy, since hardly any dishes are dirtied in the process of cooking. Surely there are some positive aspects to this, but what has been lost is more than just dirty dishes.

When it comes to food, we are exceptionally ineffective at making convincing arguments. Given that eating is so radically personal, people have all sorts of beliefs (true and false), customs and values that determine how they make food choices from day to day. But the standardization of food, the ease of pre-packaged meals and a wide lack of cooking skills has led us to a place where large portions of the population literally do not know what to eat. 'What should I eat?' is becoming an increasingly common question, as people throw up their hands at fad diets and ever-changing 'evil ingredients' that seem to change from year to year. (Is it fat? Trans fat? Sugar? Gluten? Dairy?) 'What should I eat?' is more a practical question than a moral or aesthetic one, but in fact it is incredibly loaded. It is so influenced by culture, habit, gender, race, geography, access and socio-economic status that it is hard to even construct a meaningful answer to it, never mind one with any kind of convincing general appeal. Furthermore, people have such ingrained experience with their own eating that it is hard to argue with the ideologies they have about their eating habits.

In the twenty-first century, much of the Western world seems to lack knowledge of how to eat. This is evidenced by the fact that we are as about as unhealthy as we ever have been. Three of the leading causes of death in the u.s. are heart disease, diabetes and cancer, all of which are directly impacted by the way we eat. Since the advent of processed foods (starting in the 1950s), refrigerated transit that can deliver produce, meat and dairy across long distances and to other climates, and the genetic modification of foods that can be bred for higher yields and better travel, people in the West have had access to a variety and quantity of foods unprecedented in human history. Processed sugar has become so widely available that it is almost impossible in the usa to find packaged foods that do not have processed sugar added, mostly in the form of high-fructose corn syrup. But as food becomes cheaper and more plentiful, it can also become less healthy. At the same time, we have more families with two working parents (less time to cook), more sedentary jobs and more cars. And we seem to be losing our ability to cook foods from scratch. We are suffering from a 'cultural de-skilling' – a literal lessening of the cultural knowledge required to cook. Historically, we learned to cook from our parents and other relatives. As we have moved into more than a second generation of people who do not cook regularly at home, the demand for fast food, food on the go, pre-packaged (frozen) meals and 'meal replacements' has increased substantially. These habits are taught to another generation of children, who will also become dependent on processed and pre-packaged food. Obviously there are myriad reasons why we have arrived at this point, but the overall effect is that we eat more processed foods, we eat on the go, we are heavier and more sedentary, and we are more likely to die of causes that are not unrelated to our diets and lifestyles. We also seem to find a lot less pleasure in what we eat.

It used to be the case that culture, generally speaking (and, as Michael Pollan notes, culture is just another word for your mother), would determine what people ate.[5] Culture is influenced by geography, accessibility of foods and tradition. In Mexico, for instance, corn (maize) for tortillas, beans, avocados, chilli peppers and lime (for preserving) are all relatively ubiquitous, given the physical geography of the land. Thus the bulk of Mexican cuisine is based on these foods. The terroir of a country determines the kinds of foods that are easily accessible. But when food can be delivered across continents and beyond seasons, the options become unlimited. We can eat anything, any cuisine, at any time of the year. Italian on Monday, Mexican on Tuesday, Japanese on Wednesday. But without the culture to focus the way we eat, we end up with a hodgepodge of traditions and foodstuffs. We eat cuisines that are not native and foods that are not naturally found where we live. The problem with this is that without a food culture to default to, we do not have a natural set of ingredients that can provide the kind of balance we need for a steady diet. By natural, I mean both nutritionally balanced and unprocessed. Without that, we end up fatter and less healthy.

But according to Slow Food, eating locally is not just a moral obligation but a human imperative: we should eat a certain way because it is good for our overall well-being as humans and not just as consumers. Eating Slow has implications for health, taste and economics, in addition to any kind of moral arguments one might want to make. Gregory Peterson questions whether eating locally actually does have a basis in moral obligation.[6] Peterson cites many of the arguments that have been made in the public sphere by the likes of Michael Pollan (in *The Omnivore's Dilemma*) and Barbara Kingsolver (in *Animal, Vegetable, Miracle*) about the benefits of eating locally. He catalogues the possible reasons we might have a moral obligation, but comes to the conclusion that while this is something good to do, it is not something we are obliged to do. He outlines arguments for economics, supporting family farms and businesses, environmental factors including oil used for production (fertilizers and tractors) and oil related to food miles and transportation costs. None of these seems to carry any absolute moral import, however. There are no reasons why we should eat locally (which he defines as a 100-mile radius). Supporting a family farm or a local business might be better for some, economically, but it is not clear whether this is an absolute or intrinsic good. He cites research from Peter Singer and Jim Mason, who argue that much of our environmental damage is caused by the way we factory farm, transport food and (in the u.s.) have a meat-centred diet. He dismisses these not because they are not true or relevant, but because there are ways in which these issues can be restructured to advocate fair trade, wealth distribution (to pay farmers in Madagascar a fair price for their vanilla beans, for instance) and global trade.

For Peterson, there is a straightforward argument for taste: local food supposedly tastes better than food grown at a distance. He says that the taste argument has 'intuitive appeal, since locally grown food should be fresher simply by virtue of the fact that it doesn't have to travel very far'.[7] But he then goes on to dismiss this argument, since many people live in places where food would be difficult to come by in the winter months. (He cites the total lack of fresh food available in Vermont in the winters, for example.) He muses that we should perhaps change our tastes so that we like only the food that is available, but that would be a different kind of argument. It seems to me that he misses the point of the taste argument. The taste argument is not fundamentally ethical. We have certain kinds of questions that are bound by our frameworks of history and traditions. Peterson's initial question is whether eating locally is a moral obligation. He says it is not, and within that framework I am inclined to agree with him. But that is because we do not have a clear framework within which to talk about aesthetic obligations. Taste is an aesthetic property, not a moral one. Of course, we can mean a number of different things by taste, but here I presume he means literal, gustatory taste. He says that local food presumably tastes better because it is fresher. But this is, perhaps, just an argument for fresh food, not an argument about the taste of food.

What I mean by taste here is also the literal taste of a dish (I will focus on the cooked meals rather than just raw ingredients). But fresh food will not necessarily taste better than older food. Taste – the literal taste of food – cannot have ethical obligations attached to it. Thus, even if fresh (local) food did taste better, it would not follow that we have any moral obligation to buy it, or even to prefer it. Because there are no aesthetic obligations. Obligations or duties belong to the realm of the ethical. Taste, even when one thing can be shown to taste better than another, carries no obligatory actions. Taste does impact the way we perceive the world around us, just like all our other senses do. Part of the issue is that we tend to use the concept of literal gustatory taste (tongue taste) for taste *qua* preferences and not taste *qua* flavour. Tongue taste is one of the literal ways in which we perceive the outside world, but preferences have to do with what one likes or dislikes, not whether something is salty or sweet. But what we taste (perception) influences our taste (preference).

Good taste, or tasting good, does not oblige us to buy certain foods, or even to prefer them. Finding pleasure in certain foods, which is the ultimate goal of eating good-tasting foods, provides something quite different from an obligation. It is a form of pleasure that is unique to the tongue. Perhaps gustatory pleasure is particular to humans, but not necessarily. And when philosophers have debated the subject of pleasure, it tends to be about intellectual pleasures (the highest sort of pleasure, of course). Hardly ever have philosophers taken seriously the pleasures of eating, reflection on delightful combinations of flavours, foods recalling good memories, or unique tastes that can only come from certain corners of the planet or certain traditions of cooking. Pleasure has been construed by generations of philosophers as something that is primarily associated with excess. Indulging in sexual pleasure means that you allow your body to take primary importance over your mind. Taking pleasure in alcohol means drunkenness (and hence, irrationality). Pleasure in food means gluttony – again, letting the body take control. But these biases only hold true when seen in the historical context that favours the mind over the body, and one that fears the irrationality of the body having a role in the full human experience. Thinking differently about food might help us think differently about the body as well, and maybe even about human experience.

Petrini explains that, biologically, we crave variation in our environments in order to create pleasure. A smell or taste we have every day will quickly become unnoticed, even if it is at first pleasurable (think about how a cat owner tends not to notice the smell of the litter tray as much as a guest might). But we also value routine and stability. So one way to introduce new variations of taste is to regularly try new foods. Petrini claims we need to

> broaden the range of things that give us pleasure, and
> that means learning to choose differently, even to live
> differently. From there to gastronomy is an obvious step:
> alimentary monoculture (in other words, the restricted
> range of foods and flavors experienced by those who
> simply accept what is most easily available) blanks out

the pleasures of the palate, because, no matter how much we like them, it makes them habitual.[8]

A consistent diet of the same foods over and over cannot bring us the kind of pleasure that a more varied diet can.

Terroir

Terroir has a number of different definitions, as is the case with anything so magical. For author and sommelier Bill Nesto, 'Terroir is the web that connects and unifies raw materials, their growing conditions, production processes, and the moment of product appreciation.'[9] In order to understand terroir, one must assume that the values of origin, provenance, knowledge, tradition and appreciation are all fully in place. As in many other fields, especially the art world, these values are of the utmost importance since they guarantee authenticity – that the work comes from the hand and the tradition claimed. We want to know who the artist is, since that can tell us a lot about how to interpret an artwork; we want to know when the artist was working, where they came from, who they were trained by and what they intended with the work they produced. Without these indicators, it is hard to properly appreciate the work. With art, we want to be able to attribute genius. With consumer goods, we want to be able to attribute responsibility. And with food, we want to be able to attribute quality and taste.

The notion of terroir is most commonly associated with wine. It has to do with the literal environment in which the grapes were grown. This includes the acidity of the soil, the topography of the land and the climate in any given year. All of these have a direct impact on the ways in which the grapes taste from year to year.

One of the first things wine tasters learn is how to tell the difference between Old World (most of Europe) and New World (North and South America, Australia and New Zealand) wines. New World wines are generally made in countries where viniculture had to be transplanted from the Old World, but new geography means the grapes and wines taste different. Old World wines tend to taste lighter, have less alcohol and more acidity, and taste less fruity. New World wines tend to be fruitier, with more alcohol and less acidity. Of course winemakers have a lot of control in the process, but there are still detectable differences that trained palates can identify. This has everything to do with the terroir.

Although wine is typically the product most discussed with reference to terroir, terroir impacts many food products, and it greatly affects the quality and taste of foods grown all over the world. Any foods that are not made in factories can have terroir, but as the industrialization of foods progresses, terroir diminishes as an ideal. Although terroir changes the taste of foods, for many it is more about having an origin, or a place. Often, certain flavours are only produced within a small locale and are closely associated with that place. Industrial foods are placeless, or homeless, since they have been so processed and chemically altered that the end product literally tastes the same in every season, every year. Foods that have terroir have homes, origins, makers and identifiable reasons for their flavours, and sometimes unique flaws.

For instance, a number of terroir-distinct foods are made in the northeast of Italy. Balsamic vinegar is one of the products made exclusively in Modena, in the province of Emilia-Romagna, Italy.[10] Balsamic (or Aceto Balsamico Tradizionale di Modena for top quality) is made from grape must – grapes crushed with their skins and stems. PDO balsamic is made only in Modena, in traditional ways dating back hundreds of years. The grape must juice is aged in a barrel (usually an old wine barrel) with an opening at the top, which allows air to interact with the liquid. A cheese cloth prevents insects and dust from falling in. Each year, for a minimum of seven years, the liquid is moved from one barrel to a smaller barrel as it reduces naturally in volume. The balsamic then has vinegar added to it and becomes a different product from the balsamic condiment, or the pure balsamic. Only after this extensive ageing process can the liquid be given the PDO seal, guaranteeing that it was made and cultured in Modena. Producers call the pure balsamic condiment 'black gold'.

Parmesan cheese is made in the same Italian region as the balsamic. Named after its city of origin, Parma, parmesan cheese, or, to give it its proper name, Parmigiano-Reggiano, is made only with the morning milking of the red cows who have lived in northern Italy since the fourth century AD. This is then mixed with the skimmed milk from the previous evening's milking.[11] The milk mixture is heated in copper vats, calf's rennet is added, and the collected curds are formed into a large ball, divided once, then soaked in a saltwater bath for up to three weeks. When the wheel goes into the salt bath, it is stamped with a long label that circumnavigates the entire wheel of cheese to impress upon the rind of the wheel that it is Parmigiano-Reggiano. This stamp can be seen all the way around the exterior of the large wheel, so that any portion of the wheel that is cut off shows its provenance. The same procedure allows a specific stamp with the dairy and the numbered batch of cheese, should there be any problems with the quality of the cheese later on. There is no question as to its authenticity. The cheese wheel is then taken to a drying room to age for a minimum of twelve and a maximum of 36 months. During this time, wheels are meticulously checked for cracking and bubbles (with the sound resonating from a small cheese hammer) by people who work for the dairy, as well as PDO inspectors. The wheels must be turned over regularly so that the drying process happens evenly.

Both the Parmigiano-Reggiano and the balsamic have a unique taste because of the location in which they are made – because of the microbiome, the winds, the winter, the summer, the grass, the history, the knowledge and the care with which they are made in Modena and Parma. It is impossible to make products anywhere else that taste exactly the same as these. Of course, both are made elsewhere, but not with the knowledge, standards, tradition and terroir that that are applied here. Others do not *taste* the same. The Reggio Emilia region produces the gold standard of both of these products.

Terroir is a value that can indicate the reliability of the resource chain. Parmigiano-Reggiano cheesemakers often own the cows that produce their milk, or they buy it directly from farmers who make the milk only for single cheese producers. Many Parma ham makers own their own pigs, from which they make their prosciutto. The care and feeding of the black pigs (a speciality breed used for this purpose) is of the utmost importance, since it has a significant impact on the taste of the final product. It is this taste difference that distinguishes the best breeders from the industrial ones, resulting in not just higher prices, but higher quality, better treatment of animals, workers and the land, and, of course, the tradition of excellence valued by these producers. Many winemakers also either own their own crops or buy directly from single farms. This is an essential aspect of the industry, since the quality and treatment of the base ingredients has a significant impact on the final result. Talking to these producers reveals an intense sense of pride about their products. They would not want to put their name, or their face, to a low-quality or substandard product. They express their own individuality and pride through terroir.

But terroir, especially with Parmigiano-Reggiano, is not just about individuality and taste. It is also about history. This cheese has been made exactly the same way for at least nine hundred years, making it the oldest cheese on record. The first reference to it goes all the way back to 1254, where a notary deed mentions the ownership of a parmesan cheese (*caseus parmensis*).[12] Giovanni Boccaccio also praised grated Parmigiano (*parmigiano grattugiato*) in his *Decameron* in 1348, a collection of intertwined novellas. In one of the stories, Boccaccio describes a fictional 'mountain made of grated parmigiano cheese, with people living on it who never did anything but make macaroni and ravioli and cook them in capon broth'.[13] Currently, there are only 348 Parmigiano-Reggiano dairies in the Reggio Emilia province. Importantly, each has its own history, its own family traditions and its own distinct-tasting cheese. To lump all of them together as a single taste would be like saying that all Chardonnay wines taste the same. They share a history, but they all leave their own imprint on the product as well.

Europe was one of the first regions to fully embrace food purity laws. Bavaria enacted the very first with what is known as the *Reinheitsgebot*, where beer is strictly prohibited from containing ingredients other than water, hops and barley (and later yeast). This law was first enacted in 1516 by Duke Wilhelm IV of Bavaria.[14] It soon expanded to all of Germany and has remained largely in place for the last five hundred years. For Parmigiano-Reggiano, the first purity laws came into effect in 1901. In 1909 the exact wording was finalized for the labelling of the rounds of cheese themselves. Counterfeit producers have proliferated throughout the world, and so these protections have served an important role in keeping Parmigiano-Reggiano pure. These rules include everything from prohibitions against chemical fertilization, to ensuring that the cows eat fresh grass only from spring to autumn and dried grasses from the same fields through the winter, to the number of times a day that the cheese wheels are turned and tested.[15]

Parmigiano-Reggiano is not the only cheese in the world that takes itself so seriously; nor is it the only one that shares its name with its origin. Cheddar cheese originated in Cheddar, England; Brie originated in Brie, France. Gouda comes from Gouda, Netherlands. Stilton, Roquefort and Asiago all have 'terroired' names, homes and long histories. American cheese (also known as 'pasteurized cheese product'), on the other hand, comes from American factories. In fact, it is not even legally allowed to be called cheese, since there is no cheese in it. Not incidentally, this is the kind of cheese McDonald's uses on its burgers. Other industrial cheeses, such as mozzarella (not fresh buffalo mozzarella, which is made in Italy from water buffalo milk), are also made from a number of different varieties of cow's milk. The cows who produce the milk eat primarily a diet of silage, which can come from any number of places and includes a large amount of corn or processed corn. The cheese is made in highly sterilized factories that produce tons of generic-tasting industrial cheese a year. This cheese is consistent throughout the country. Importantly, though, part of what makes cheese special is the fermenting bacteria that give different flavours, the milk that is distinctive of the land, and the traditions of the cheesemakers. Industrial cheese is really a scientific concoction that resembles cheese but cannot share any kind of meaningful history. American 'Parmesan cheese' does not adhere to the PDO designation, and since there is very little regulation for it outside Italy, it can be sold in a wide range of forms, including our most familiar one, ready-grated parmesan in a green can. The ideals of Slow Food require recognition that food comes from the earth, the plants and animals who inhabit it and the skilled craftspeople who make it. It does not come from industrial factories. Slow Food aspires to value the products that *connect* us to the land, not those that are nameless and placeless.

The idea of terroir is originally, and decidedly, French. Historical documents indicate that the French, perhaps more than any other nationality, associate themselves with the land and the places where they dwell in a fundamental way. In her book *The Taste of Place*, Amy Trubeck explains how this way of thinking 'always begins with a defined place, tracing the taste of place back from the mouth to the plants and animals and ultimately into the soil.'[16] In France, she says, terroir is a 'category that frames[s] perceptions and practices – a worldview, or should we say a foodview.'[17] When food is thought to be 'grounded' and the actual taste is connected to the people and traditions, the ways in which community is generated is radically different from if the food is placeless and thereby meaningless.

Slow Food wants to acknowledge the traditions and localities that food comes from, but I do not consider it necessary to take an absolute position on this, especially in our globalized world where so many foods are hard to source locally. But there surely is something to be said for food that is uniquely connected to the land as being an expression of the land itself, as well as the people who cultivate that land. Lisa Heldke contextualizes this issue nicely when she proposes a third way between the dichotomy of (hyper-)localism and globalism. She begins with an anecdote about the city of Lucca, Italy, where the municipal council ruled that 'with a view to safeguarding culinary traditions and the authenticity of structure, architecture, culture and history, establishments whose activities can be tracked to different ethnicities won't be allowed to operate in the center of town.'[18] Heldke's analysis begins with a consideration of what this kind of ruling would mean for a town. Ultimately, it enforces a kind of regulated localism, or what Heldke calls 'strategic authenticity', if not with actual food products, then with food types and traditions. In this particular case, it seems to have been a specific targeting of kebab shops that were run by immigrants, not McDonald's and their standardized food conglomerates.

Heldke positions this form of hyper-localism, on which the political decisions were made, in opposition to cosmopolitanism or globalism. She borrows a definition from Josiah Royce where localism (or, for Royce, provincialism) is constituted by 'the love and pride which leads the inhabitants of a province to cherish as their own [those] traditions, beliefs and aspirations [with which a province is associated]'.[19] This kind of love and pride can be seen all over the world, especially in smaller or more remote communities that have been somewhat isolated from the impacts of broader influences. Cosmopolitanism, on the other hand, understood by Anthony Appiah, is constituted by two ideals that tend to be tightly woven together: first, 'the idea that we have obligations to others . . . that stretch beyond those to whom we are related', and second, 'that we take seriously the value not just of human life, but of particular human lives, which means taking an interest in the practices and beliefs that lend them significance.'[20] Thus cosmopolitanism forces us to recognize that we have obligations to others, and to particular others that go well beyond our family and small community. Looking at the subtleties of these two concepts is the task for another book, but they are firmly entrenched in the ways in which we think about food, and in the way we eat. Often, it seems as though we need to make a choice about which of these we value, since it seems impossible to value the close and the far simultaneously. Heldke proposes that these are not the only two ways in which we can think about food. There is, in fact, a more realistic third way, she proposes. The reason a third way is needed, she says, is because the world we now inhabit is neither radically local nor entirely cosmopolitan. She suggests that we adopt the position of what she calls a 'nested traveler', recognizing that we coexist in grounded places, but that we also interact in meaningful ways with people from the outside. With this third way, one can value the traditions of one's people and place, but also connect with the more global foods, cultures and peoples that travel in and out of our lives.

Although Heldke is not talking about Slow Food, she is talking about the ways in which respect for home, soil, tradition and dinner can, at the same time, respect tradition *and* grow to be more inclusive. Despite some of the ways we think about traditional recipes or ancient foodways, food traditions are still organic, in that they are always growing and changing. Traditional recipes *started* at some point, but traditions develop and grow given the realities of economic change, changes of taste, access to food resources and development. So while terroir is something we can taste, community is what builds food customs. Place is where food traditions begin, but people are what make food meaningful.

Community

Part of the Slow Food ideology is that eating together is an essential aspect of having a healthy food culture. Shared meals should be a natural part of the work of Slow Food. Foods grown, gathered, bought and prepared deserve an appreciative audience. Sociology can tell us about the social habits of groups, and the ways in which inequities are seen clearly around meals. Anthropology can tell us about the traditions of different cultures and peoples in the ways that they share meals. But philosophy can tell us about how the ways people eat are to do with the latent beliefs and values that they have around food and sharing. Given that most people are largely not aware of ideological beliefs, it is important to understand how these can influence the ways we behave in the world.

Given that eating is shared universally among humans, our eating practices really do tell us a lot about the ways we think about food. Different cultures have different customs at the table, but what is universal is that we all have shared meals, we all have tables, and shared meals always have some understood structure and set of social rules. Eating together is one of the many ways in which we connect with others as we nourish ourselves and share our tables with friends. Eating together is an essential part of what Slow Food is. But eating together should be the culmination of a process of understanding – it is not *just* about eating together. As Wendell Berry has said, 'Eating is an agricultural act.'[21] This means that eating is the end of a long process that involves planting, cultivating, harvesting, transporting, selling, cooking and serving. Eating should include a recognition of the animals that have been sacrificed, the labour that was involved in getting food to the plate and the hands that prepared the food. For hundreds of years this was the default way most people ate, because so much time and effort went into getting food to their bellies.

But we are now in a time where consumerism has taken over the way we think of everything. Where the ideals of efficiency and cheap labour work well in some sectors of society, they tend to have an adverse effect when it comes to the way we eat. We have instituted 'Fordization' to our food, implementing factory production lines to create what Michael Pollan calls 'edible foodlike substances'.[22] Consumer eating, as Berry calls it, allows consumers to be merely passive. We pay (mostly) whatever we are charged, and 'mostly ignore certain critical questions about the quality and the cost of what they are sold: How fresh is it? How pure or clean is it, how free of dangerous chemicals? How far was it transported, and what did transportation add to the cost? How much did manufacturing or packaging or advertising add to the cost?' and so on.[23] Processed foods theoretically began in a field, but have a very different life from foods that come direct from fields and farmers. They also have a very different transportation life, which can often involve trips to several countries before finding their way to our supermarket shelves.[24] Many processed foods barely resemble the foods they originally came from.

But much of our culture today values convenience, ease and simplicity. Food that does not have to be 'cooked' at all is of the utmost value since it involves no skill and very little time. Those meals come from factories, not farms. Food from farms, with its chain of production involving farmers, not food scientists, requires more work and a speciality knowledge of how to prepare various dishes. Berry's point is that this kind of food, when we eat with the awareness that eating is an agricultural act, connects us to the land in a way that processed food cannot. When we are disconnected from the land, we become disconnected from our surroundings in a much more profound way. Berry explains that, like with 'industrial sex, industrial eating has become a degraded, poor, paltry thing. Our kitchens and other eating places more and more resemble filling stations, as our homes more and more resemble motels.'[25] There is no moral obligation as such to eat at home, but eating together with others adds to the connection that food can provide us with. There are lots of ways to do it, but some are more fulfilling than others.

In Adam Gopnik's delightful book *The Table Comes First*, he develops an entire argument beginning with the one presupposition, the one value, that the dining room table is the first purchase that a young couple should make, given that it is the centre of family life. 'The table comes first,' he says, 'before the meal and even before the kitchen where it's made. It precedes everything in remaining the one plausible hearth of family life, the raft to ride down the river of existence even in the hardest times.'[26] Gopnik suggests that given the centrality of food to our lives, the table is also the centrepiece of drama, pain, romance and all the 'big fights about who we are – our notions of clan and nation, identity and the individual.'[27] The table is central to families big and small, and the development of community happens not only around the table but with the sharing of food. Of course, eating together also allows people to demonstrate many of the most important virtues of generosity, hospitality and moderation.

I need to mention that not all people can cook at home. Some cannot afford family meals; some people work so hard and so long that meals at a table are never an option. Kids have busy schedules that do not always allow for regular meals. What I am saying, and what advocates of Slow Food promote, is not about shaming people, especially women, for not cooking enough. It is about thinking about the entire food system in a different way. Many people *could* do this kind of buying and cooking but choose not to. My suggestion is that pleasure, community and a connection to nature are lost when the foods we eat come from factories and farms. Children are short-changed when they cannot recognize foods in their natural state. It becomes difficult for them to understand how basic science works, the realities of where 'chicken nuggets' come from, and how a different economy is possible when farmers are paid directly at the market. When people buy goods from the very people who grow and make those goods, relationships are formed and trust is generated. No such relationships can exist when dozens of middlemen handle all the transactions between farmers and buyers.

In his book *In Defense of Food*, food journalist Michael Pollan argues that people should eat 'food' (which, as a general guideline, he gives as having five ingredients or fewer, all of which you can pronounce or, more generally, your grandmother would recognize as food). He encourages people to cook more and to buy less processed and fast food. He wrote another book, *Cooked*, about the history of the four primary forms of cooking (fire, water, air and earth), or transforming food into more digestible and more palatable meals.[28] He was criticized from a number of directions for his suggestions being too upper-middle class, too white and too masculine. For who other than a white upper-middle-class woman would have the time to make things from scratch and cook elaborate meals for her family? Rachel Laudan, a vocal critic of the Slow Food movement as well as of Pollan himself, argues that 'human food is processed food. And there are good reasons for this. Overall, processed foods are easier to eat and digest, more nutritious, tastier, safer, and longer lasting. The idea that any change made in the raw material is detrimental is just flat wrong.'[29] Laudan wrote a controversial piece defending what she calls 'culinary modernism', where she suggests that the processed food that the likes of Michael Pollan and Carlo Petrini (among others) shun is a modern miracle, and not at all out of line with the values that have shaped so much of the modern world.[30] Much of this debate is around the goodness and badness of the processed food industry, and whether or not one can become virtuous through cooking ingredients one finds at the farmer's market. This does not need to be a moral argument so much as one to do with awareness, and the understanding of the ways in which food plays a role in many aspects of our lives that we have forgotten about as a culture.

It is not all about forgetting. Our food system has been transformed over the last several decades in both good and bad ways. We have access to a considerable variety of foods we did not before. We have access to fresh foods in all seasons. Foods last considerably longer than they did because of the development of preservatives. The industrial meat economy is hidden behind 'ag-gag' laws that do not allow a transparent understanding of the way meat is processed, marketing allows only eight multinational companies to own 90 per cent of all food labels,[31] and there is a complete misunderstanding of government regulations having to do with expiration dates, sell-by dates and food quality. Nutritional information that changes from year to year about eggs, bacon, milk, gluten, fat, sugar and so on have led consumers to believe that they need nutrition scientists to help them with diet choices. But we get to the point where we are confused because of the nutrition scientists, and because of the vast quantity of processed food and fast food that permeates our food landscape.

One of the most memorable meals I ever had in Italy was just a couple of tomatoes, cut in half, face down in a pan of water, slow cooked over low heat, two sprigs of fresh basil, pasta from a box and a sprinkling of salt. I begged my host for the recipe. She said it wasn't complicated, but it would take some time. When she told me how she had made it, I was astounded. It was so simple. But most Slow Food is simple. And it requires good ingredients to start with. I could not make that recipe with a tomato from my supermarket, though, since they are hothouse tomatoes bred to travel. They don't taste good, and they don't have the same acidity that heirloom varieties need to make that kind of sauce. It is important not to conflate Slow Food with complicated food. The typical Italian cuisine that formed the basis of Slow Food is peasant food that comes from the staples of the land – wheat for pizza and bruschetta, corn for polenta and whatever happens to be available for topping both of them.

Conversations around food these days are more than plentiful, as eaters, dieters, lay nutritionists and even authors grasp at the best way to eat, which foods to cut out, which foods to focus on and the evil ingredients of the day. But people have been eating food from the land for, well, ever. Slow Food is merely a way of organizing the attempt not to be taken over completely by industrial food and fast life. Slow Food and Slow Life are not moral mandates or commandments. People who do not choose to live this way can be perfectly happy, but it is a *way of life*, or what philosophers call a *world view*, inclusive of all of the parts of the agricultural system – growing, purchasing, cooking, and eating together. It can provide its own form of pleasure, connect us as humans, and feed us, body and soul.

4

Food Fraud and Authenticity

Philosophers, especially philosophers of art, have long had an interest in fraud. Fraudulent paintings have captured the imaginations of readers and museum patrons who wonder just how we can tell the difference between the real thing and a fake. What is at stake can be a lot of money, but there is also a sense that originals convey something much more special than a fake; they provide us with a connection to their makers, originality and the ever-elusive 'authenticity'. Some might even say that those originals have an aura about them.[1] In some cases, only trained experts can tell the difference between the authentic and the fake, but there might be other ways of showing, or knowing.

Is there such a thing as fraudulent food? How can we tell the difference between authentic food and fake food? Is there such a thing as fake food? Not authentic cuisine *per se* (such as 'authentic Italian'), but rather authentic ingredients, like extra virgin olive oil, wine from a particular region or winery, or whether or not certain flavours use real ingredients or have been chemically enhanced – like almost anything that is 'truffle'-flavoured. With food, knowledge comes primarily from tasting, but also from various beliefs that we have about where it came from, or what it is, or what it is supposed to be. Reading labels provides a foundation for those beliefs, but labels can be misleading: they can exaggerate and even lie. Labels may not be a good source of reliable knowledge about food at all, since they also reduce nutritional information into relatively meaningless percentages and quantities measured in scientific terms. Taste can supply us with a form of knowledge that cannot come from any other sense. Our sense of taste is arguably an important vehicle for knowledge that we have radically underdeveloped, because of the way we have privileged vision and hearing over taste and smell in terms of the way we construct knowledge.

There is a strong tie, both historically and linguistically, between vision and knowledge. In ancient Greek, *oida*, the verb 'to see', is *eidos*, 'to know', in its past tense. So after one sees, one knows. *Eidos* is, of course, the word Plato uses that we translate as 'form' or 'idea'. Heraclitus was the first to call vision the *best* of the senses, when he said that 'eyes are more exact witnesses than ears'.[2] Plato uses the visual analogy of light in the allegory of the cave as being the manifestation of understanding; without the ability to leave the cave and 'see the light' one cannot know. Ideas allow things to appear clearly, just as light helps to illuminate objects. For him, sight is the lens between the outer world and the inner mind, and the only sense that can allow us to have objective knowledge about the outside world. Aristotle proclaims in his *Metaphysics* that 'all men desire to know', and then remarks specifically on how we *delight* in vision more than the other senses, for its own sake, in addition to its usefulness.[3] Our primary vehicle for knowledge is vision.

Descartes, one of the founders of the science of optics, took the eye to be a completely passive lens, but one that separated the physical and the metaphysical, the corporeal world and the mind. Sight is tied to light and space, the clearest manifestation of the corporeal world, while hearing is tied to sound and time. Sight gives us objective knowledge, and much of what we call reliable epistemology is dependent upon sight rather than any of the other senses. Currently, we still value vision as our primary vehicle for knowing something to be the case.[4]

Hearing does come in at a close second in terms of the senses that produce reliable or 'objective' knowledge, since it is also information gained at a distance. Since vision and hearing both work with separation from our physical bodies, we are able to have relevantly similar experiences to other people in close proximity. Vision and hearing are called the 'distal' senses, ones that we use from a distance. But taste is drastically different. We do not *know* things from tasting, but rather, taste is something that gives us only preferences and likings, or perhaps sense experiences that cannot be reflected upon. Sight can give us knowledge, the kind of knowledge philosophers have given preference to since the beginning: objective knowledge, or what I might as well call here visual-objective knowledge. It might go too far to say that vision dictated much of philosophical epistemology, but I do not think it an overstep to say that vision and epistemology are absolutely co-dependent.

Much of aesthetics, despite the fact that we focus on the experiences of the senses, is dependent on a cognitivist approach, as well as one that favours the visual. That is, aesthetic *appreciation* requires some sort of cognitive content or belief in order to make sense of the aesthetic pleasure that we experience. To put it this way, our capacity for taste provides sensations, but not cognitive content; feeling, but not thought. Or so the objections go. But the objections might not be so strong if we did not value sight so highly above the other senses. Maybe other senses can give us different kinds of knowledge from the vision-centred theories.

Taste, touch and smell are called our 'proximal senses', since we use our bodies directly to experience the world with them. Georg Hegel, for instance, claimed that our 'lower senses' (taste, touch and smell) were even incapable of providing artistic experiences since they were practical and not theoretical, and thus incapable of providing information to the imagination.[5] These lower senses cannot give us anything, then, other than bodily sensation that produces nothing for us to think about (in terms of content) or contemplate (in terms of the imagination). Kant asserts that matters of gustatory taste or flavour can be agreeable but not beautiful. They can be agreeable to me, but not beautiful to everyone, since matters of gustatory taste are mere sensations. Mere flavours and aromas, he says, along with 'mere colour' and 'mere tone are relegated to judgements of agreeableness, because they have as their ground merely the matter of the sensations, namely mere sensation.'[6] He is a formalist when it comes to matters of beauty: the *form* contributes to the representation of an object, but not the *matter*, or the pure aesthetic sensations. Sensations are necessary to be able to have aesthetic judgements, but the possibility of contemplation about them is what makes it possible to universalize them and to make them command universal assent. Thus we cannot derive knowledge from the lower senses, or any mere sensations, and we cannot make aesthetic claims about those sensations. Significantly, neither Kant, nor Hume, nor Hegel allow taste, or food or drink, to be considered anything but *mere* sensation.

Kant and Hume both relied on this distinction between the higher and the lower concerning the senses when they emphasized the disinterestedness that comes in contemplating aesthetic properties, and both came to the general conclusion that taste cannot be considered aesthetic since there is no way to reflect on it disinterestedly. They both valued the disinterested approach to aesthetic objects, suggesting that aesthetic objects must be given space – physical space – to be contemplated properly. The space would be akin to the physical space that allows us to *see* objects, or *hear* sounds. Given that these philosophers have provided so much of the foundational structure of the way we make sense of aesthetics, their concerns cannot be dismissed out of hand. But they have provided us with a foundational structure that is predisposed towards the epistemology of vision, which unnecessarily denigrates sensual pleasure. We are not merely minds, but also bodies, and we experience the world in many sensory ways. Our theories of aesthetic appreciation should reflect full bodily sensation and the uses of all of our bodily senses. As it is, most aesthetic theory is still focused on aesthetic pleasure that is contemplative or cognitive.

The notion of taste in aesthetics is used more widely in its metaphorical sense – in the sense of liking or finding pleasure in certain kinds of objects – than for literally tasting food. Our senses of taste and smell can warn us of rotten or poisonous food, but they also help us to experience the world around us, especially in culturally specific surroundings. For this reason, taste and smell are essential vehicles for meaning-making. We are not just passive receptacles for food; taste can inform us about our world in very precise, and even unique, ways. We take the external and make it internal, or we make the objective the subjective, passing it right over our tongues. When we eat, we learn what something tastes like; we gain knowledge that we could not gain from even the most detailed description. Although not all tasting is aesthetic, tasting can be appreciated aesthetically in ways that we have not allowed it to be, given our dominant historical framework. Taste can give us pleasure, both bodily and contemplative, and it can also give us knowledge.

But is there a model for appreciating food? The philosopher Allen Carlson has outlined a number of models for appreciating nature that might work with food as well. He outlines what he calls an object-centred model and a landscape model. Since appreciating nature is not the same as appreciating art, and most of the accounts of appreciation are specifically about art, we need to expand that a bit. The object-centred model is one where 'we actually or contemplatively remove the object from its surroundings and dwell on its sensuous design qualities and its possible expressive qualities'.[7] This kind of appreciation allows serious contemplation of a single work or artefact, so that its expressive, representational, formal or aesthetic qualities can be foregrounded and the work can be contemplated without the distraction of context. This is something museums do for art objects generally; they provide a contemplative space where appreciators can focus on a work. Carlson says this is not a good approach, since context is so important for understanding nature, and things taken from their environments can have drastically changed meanings.

The landscape model, which takes a static view of a landscape (think of what you might see through the lens of a telescope or even in a photo or a painting), is bounded and only two-dimensional. When appreciating nature this seems to lack something essential in appreciating the environment, which has incredible depth and richness. For Carlson, this is not a good model, because this encourages the viewer to appreciate the environment 'not as what it is and with the qualities it has, but rather as something which it is not and with qualities it does not have'.[8] He advocates a third approach, which he calls the environmental model. With this approach, one chooses to focus on a particular foreground and makes a conscious decision on what to keep in the background. We can 'select certain foci of aesthetic significance and perhaps exclude others, thereby limiting the experience'.[9] Otherwise, we end up focusing on everything, and nothing is experienced with deep appreciation.

Carlson talks about ways in which standard models of appreciating art are used when appreciating nature, but how do these work with food? For me, the object model actually works quite well. Food taken out of context and into exclusive focus can be delighted in and savoured. Food appreciated this way can be the focus of identification exercises and taste tests. Single foods can be appreciated for bringing back memories of childhood favourites and first dates. The object model of food appreciation can be quite satisfying. The landscape model translates well to the way we *look* at food and appreciate its visual qualities. We like meals that are plated artistically, ones whose colours are bright or deep, and meals that look delicious. We always 'eat with our eyes first' and so food needs to look appealing. Carlson's environmental model is actually the one that I think works best for appreciating food. With this, food is supplemented by an understanding of source, cooking techniques, flavours, textures, balance and, most importantly, taste. One can choose what to focus on and what to background, but they are conscious choices. There are lots of ways that we don't appreciate what we eat, by not paying attention to *any* of these. We all do this regularly, but in an attempt to understand how we can have knowledge of food, we need to understand more than one way that we can appreciate it.

The philosopher Matteo Ravasio outlines a list of requirements that a model of food appreciation should meet, based on Carlson's environmental model.[10] He lists the following as being important aspects to focus on: intentionality, historicity, normativity, authenticity, appropriation and meaning.[11] These categories cover a wide range of aspects of food production, preparation and contextualization. But, ironically, he does not include *taste* as one of the required categories for the appreciation of food. This list approaches food mostly as a cultural artefact and not as an object of taste, a source of pleasure or a prompt for contemplation. But if taste becomes the focus, we can set aside the visual aspects and the historical-cultural aspects just for a moment, so we can develop a better theory of taste. We could focus on flavour, balance and texture, but not animal cruelty, unfair labour practices, the various regions where foods might be grown or even to whose recipes or cultural traditions the food may belong. This kind of account is more focused on what we might call the formal elements of tasting, instead of the contextual ones that try to dictate what things are *supposed* to taste like, rather than what they *actually* taste like.

If our appreciation of food was primarily based on taste, we could begin to develop *trust* in taste that we currently may not have. We would be able to identify different flavours and sensations, and begin to detect the differences in quality between fresh and stale herbs and spices, for instance. We could develop a sense of taste that was more and more discriminating, in the same way that trained art historians learn to be able to identify different styles and techniques of painting. But for the most part, we do not do much to cultivate our sense of taste. This is partly because taste is a bodily sense and it can vary so much from person to person. Additionally, we do not learn to trust taste since it cannot give us objective knowledge – that is, knowledge that we can see and evaluate from a distance. If we cultivated this trust in taste, we would be able to more readily identify different flavours and variations of those flavours, such as with olive oil. But, as I said earlier, aesthetic appreciation is different from knowledge, and I am aiming for the latter. Appreciation is most generally to do with beauty and understanding the nature of art, but here it is really focused on the ways in which we find pleasure in certain kinds of aesthetic experiences. Aesthetic knowledge, however, has to do with some of the more 'objective' ways of thinking about aesthetic experiences, and the ways in which we understand, conceptualize and maybe even learn from aesthetic experiences. Remember, epistemology is dominated by the visual, and it is hard even to speak of ways in which we can *know* through taste, touch and smell. But the aesthetic supposedly focuses on sensation more generally. So it seems to be the time to give taste its own account.

It is also important to be able to move seamlessly between food and drink, and taste. It seems wrong to talk about taste in the abstract, or food in the abstract, without talking about particular instances, since the experiences tend to be so drastically different. Food can be considered in countless ways: a commodity to be bought and sold, fuel for our bodies; it can be expressive of a particular culture or a parent's love for their children. What we *know* about food in these ways reverts back to objective or propositional knowledge: how much courgettes cost per kilo, where they were grown, how much I need to eat to feel full, what kind of traditional dishes are made in Mexico City, or the kind of biscuits my mother made for me when I was young. One of the other ways in which food can be approached is the way it tastes. It can be too salty, spicy or heavy, but different foods have particular flavours that we expect and experience from them. But how does food taste? Is it only a generic description that we might allow? Sweet? Salty? Bitter? There are general categories like these (sweet, salty, bitter, sour and umami) but there are also specific flavours, such as lemon, cucumber or anise. Individual foods can taste sour or like lemon, but I cannot know that particular taste without first-hand experience. I can know that lemons are sour, but I cannot know what lemons taste like without tasting them. If I only know they are sour, I might not be able to differentiate between a lemon and a lime, say, or a lemon and a battery. Without tasting I cannot differentiate between a Meyer, Eureka or Lisbon lemon. Just because I have an abstract concept or idea of the taste of a lemon does not mean I can identify it merely by looking at it. So the tongue, and taste, gives us a kind of experience that we do not get from any of our other senses. Why might this count as knowledge and not, as Kant might say, mere sensation or just perception? Knowledge, for Kant, is cognitive, not sensory; but Kant's view really is dictated by a very narrow account of what counts as knowledge.

Truth, Lies and Olive Oil

In order to demonstrate why it is important to develop a philosophical account of taste, let us consider olive oil – genuine extra virgin olive oil. The health benefits of real extra virgin olive oil are tremendous and one of the primary reasons that people who eat a Mediterranean diet have such a low incidence of heart disease. Olive oil has been used to treat indigestion, nappy rash, infertility, dry hair and chapped lips, and has even been thought to cure depression. Further studies show that it can reduce the risk of cancer and Alzheimer's disease.[12] Even today, many Italians drink a shot of olive oil every morning as a part of a health regimen. Gary Beauchamp, former director of the Monell Chemical Senses Center in Philadelphia, noticed that the burning sensation at the back of the throat when one swallows good olive oil is similar to the burning one gets when one chews a tablet of ibuprofen. After much scientific experimentation, he discovered that it is the same molecule that causes that burn in both the olive oil and the ibuprofen. As it turns out, olive oil has the same anti-inflammatory properties as ibuprofen.[13] As a natural anti-inflammatory, it helps with chronic pain, which is the reason that it can reduce the risk of heart disease.

Philosophical research on taste, if it is about food or drink, tends to be done almost exclusively on wine. Wine is perhaps the most potentially *complex* of the liquids we ingest, but it is also something we drink mostly in order to taste it, to accompany good food or for reasons to do with social lubrication. Olive oil is common in much of our food and dressings without our realizing it. Italians, especially southern Italians, use it to cook meat and potatoes, in baked goods, ice cream and countless other foods. It enhances the flavours of many different foods, from salad to chocolate cake. Olive oil was and is still one of the most important substances in much of the Mediterranean, where it is used for cooking, skin care, hair growth, heart ailments, religious purposes, trade, deodorant and as a basis for perfumes and lamp oil (*lepante* in Italian). But it has some important complexities and variations as well. Like many foods, olive oil can have exceptional terroir – that is, aspects of geography, elevation, weather, soil conditions and climate that impact its taste dramatically. The subtle variations in the oil can only be determined by tasting.

Perhaps somewhat surprisingly, olive oil has an extremely chequered past. The first record of olive oil fraud, where cheaper and lower-quality oils were used to cut the pure olive oil, was over two thousand years ago. This is the first instance of *any* sort of food fraud on record. In artefacts from ancient Greece and Rome, hundreds of thousands of olive oil 'amphorae show evidence of extensive fraud measures: each [amphora] was painted with the exact weight of oil it contained, along with the name of the farm where the olives were pressed, the merchant who shipped the oil, and the official who verified this information before shipment'.[14] Mount Testaccio in Rome, a literal mountain of ancient olive oil containers, is a treasure trove of history that allows us access to the ancient Roman olive oil industry. Each terracotta amphora gives information about the contents of its oil. In ancient times, people bought on average 50 litres of oil a year, and spent on it what we might spend on petrol. It was an incredibly important commodity, and because of its value it was also rife with the potential for fraud. Based on the amphorae that we have, it is also clear that governments, sellers and consumers anticipated the fraud and took extensive measures to stop it.

Much of the world's supply of olive oil has been tampered with. There are three primary ways in which extra virgin olive oil can be changed. Lesser-quality oils such as rapeseed, peanut, soya and 'vegetable' oil are added to pure olive oil to increase the volume without radically impacting the colour or viscosity, but they usually lessen the peppery flavour and the health benefits. Second, the extra virgin oil can be diluted with lower grades of actual olive oil. This makes an acidity test almost impossible to apply since the acidity is so similar. Third, producers can manufacture oil at the very low end of the regulatory spectrum, using old olives and adding old oil from previous years that has been held in storage for long periods.[15] Some estimates are that as much as 80 per cent of the world production of olive oil is cut with cheaper oils, lessening the benefits of its consumption.[16] Other estimates are that only 2 per cent of the olive oil that is sold is really top-tier, extra virgin olive oil.[17] But olive oil is a substance that one cannot know the quality of without extensive knowledge of taste, at least of some premium oils. Chemical tests are unreliable since they only measure the chemical and acidity levels (0.08 per cent at most for extra virgin) of the oil and cannot determine anything about the origin or quality of the fruit. Chemical tests cannot determine tastes. Recently, the Italian government has taken anti-fraud measures by requiring Italian producers to sell oil in glass bottles that are not refillable – they have a built-in device which only allows the oil to flow out. By the end of the twentieth century, according to one EU investigator, olive oil was considered the most adulterated agricultural product in the European Union, with the potential profits comparable to cocaine trafficking but 'none of the risks'.[18]

But there *are* risks to bad oil, and the worst is death. In 1981 in Spain there was an outbreak of what has been called 'toxic oil syndrome', in which over twenty thousand people died after ingesting fraudulent olive oil made from rapeseed oil denatured with aniline, 'a highly toxic organic compound used to manufacture plastics'.[19] This is the worst case in recorded history. You might not die from a cut-price product, but neither will you reap the many health or flavour benefits of this almost magical substance. What might be (philosophically) worse is that we develop false beliefs about what olive oil tastes like and thus make faulty judgements based on these false beliefs.

Good olive oil should smell peppery, bitter, fruity and like fresh olives. Olive oil is the only kind of oil that is made with the flesh of the olive, rather than the stone, from which most other plant-based oils are made. Olive oil is really a form of fruit juice and does not get better with age, like wine and balsamic do. Olive oil degrades over time and with sunlight, so good olive oil is always sold in darkened glass. The benefits of olive oil are greatest when it is fresh, and oil that is more than a year old is often not good: the health benefits diminish and the taste suffers. Moreover, there are sixteen official taste flaws, as determined by the EU: fusty, musty, muddy, vinegary, metallic, rancid, burnt, hay, rough, greasy, vegetable water, brine, grassy, earthy, grubby and cucumber. If any of these flaws are detected the olive oil cannot be sold to high-end producers. No chemical tests can detect these, only humans.

Extra virgin olive oil is one of the first designations given by the European parliament as a legal grade of oil. The law, passed in 1960, required that extra virgin oil be made 'solely by mechanical methods, without chemical treatment, and set a number of chemical requirements, including a maximum of 1 per cent free acidity'.[20] The acid levels are one of the primary factors in assessing quality oil from *lepante* (lamp oil), which is not fit for human consumption. The difference between extra virgin and *lepante* is only 1 per cent. Furthermore, it cannot have any taste flaws, and must have 'some perceptible fruitiness'.[21] And, according to journalist Tom Mueller, 'with this law olive oil became the first food in the world – and to this day one of a mere handful – whose quality was legally determined at least in part by its taste'.[22] But given that so much of the production is adulterated either by cheaper oils or by heat, many people would not know how to identify real olive oil given the opportunity. Many Americans have actually become accustomed to olive oil that is rancid, since most of what is sold there has already gone bad (of course, most people don't drink it straight, either!). If it hasn't gone bad, the olive oil we buy in the supermarket is likely to be denatured, heated or treated with chemicals to lessen the natural flavour. But we can't *taste* the difference because we don't *know* the difference. If extra virgin oil can produce the health benefits that the Italians and Greeks claim, then we are being taken advantage of, paying for medicine and receiving snake oil.

So how do we stave off that fraud? Certainly we can't all become expert olive oil tasters. Except we can. Opportunities abound if one knows where to look for classes (these do exist), olive oil bars and even oil presses. Intentional tasting can allow one to begin to *learn* what good oil tastes like. As with visual art, learning to taste carefully doesn't happen in a day, but regular exposure and intentional comparisons can easily lead to a more refined ability to taste, and thus to know, good oil. Our tongues can distinguish vast differences and also very subtle distinctions between different foods and liquids, but philosophers at least have not always given the sense of taste full credit since there may not be cognitive content associated with the sense. I might here be accused of elitism, having recommended olive-oil-tasting classes, but it is just an example of one of the ways we can begin to pay attention to taste – all taste. Olive oil just happens to have a commodity market that is heavily fraudulent and so works well as an example. I do not need to argue that there is cognitive content, but rather that the kind of knowledge taste can provide is something that can be cultivated, developed, learned and eventually known.

Cultivating Taste and Knowledge

So why have we had such a mistrust in taste? Because it is subjective, and it is of the body. And the historical context that we work within just does not allow it. We make better use of taste in its metaphorical use than the literal. Gustatory taste is often something we have not intentionally cultivated reliable knowledge about. If we did, we might be able to tell the difference between real olive oil and fake – because we would have experience and then knowledge of it. We would know the difference not because we read a label or see the colour, but because we know it with our tongue. Our tongue and only our tongue can compare flavours to other oils we have tasted before, and can put them in context with other tastes that we also know. If we were able to break away from the epistemology of the vision paradigm that we have inherited from our philosophical ancestors, we might be able to trust in taste in ways that we have refused to before. This is not something we need to leave to the experts, any more than we need to leave the appreciation of art to the art historians. Cultivating and training can lead to better judgements, less fraud, more pleasure, understanding and articulation of preferences and, most importantly, more reliable taste knowledge.

Barry C. Smith provides some useful terminology here. He suggests that *tastes* are properties of a certain food or drink. *Tasting* is an experience one has. Taste is of an object; tasting is a subjective experience.[23] Tastes are *in* foods and drinks (and oil) whether we perceive them or not. Smith explains, 'Tastes are properties . . . that give rise to certain experiences in us; and they cannot be reduced to, or equated with, those experiences.'[24] It is worth adopting his terminology here, so as not to mistake the object for the experience. Although it seems to be awfully easy to conflate the two, given the slipperiness of the language, it is a distinction that is useful in my larger argument, which is to do with the way we move from ignorant taster to expert connoisseur.

This raises some important philosophical questions about taste, specifically about whether we start with assumptions that are realist or idealist. Is taste something in the mind or does it exist in an external object? If it is something in the mind, then it would be virtually impossible to have objective knowledge about various foods, since it would all be completely subjective and dependent on personal experience alone. If we approach our theory of taste as realists, then it would be seemingly impossible to gain access to that knowledge, since we have to ingest (or destroy) the food in order to know at first hand what it tastes like. This is not the case with objects of vision, since the object of perception is not impacted by our perceiving it. But because taste is inherently subjective, it seems that we cannot have objective knowledge of it at all. And yet that does not seem right. There are all kinds of (aesthetic) properties that are inherent in objects of consideration, and people are regularly able to identify these properties with high levels of agreement. This is, presumably, what sommeliers do with great consistency – identify 'objective' properties that are in various wines. These sommeliers seem to be able to consistently identify properties in various foods and drink. We might even call them objective qualities that Smith would call *tastes*. Sommeliers have trained themselves to be able to detect *tastes* in food and drink in a way that makes us think that *tasting* can be an objective experience in just the way seeing is. And, of course, people can be experts – sommeliers, in fact – at identifying these properties not only of wine, but of cheese, beer, water, coffee, milk, sake and even olive oil.

We might go down the route of talking about extrinsic and intrinsic qualities. Extrinsic qualities are described as the way something tastes in terms of being flowery, fresh, lemony or cucumbery. The categorization of a flavour as 'lemony', for example, is a mental connection between the taste of an oil and lemons, but there is no actual lemon in the oil. Intrinsic qualities are qualities that are inherent *in* the oil that we can only experience with our sense of taste. We cannot perceive them by looking at them and it is impossible to perceive them without tasting directly. Intrinsic qualities of olive oil would be about the mouthfeel of the oil, the level of spiciness (or in the case of good olive oil, pepperiness), or how long the flavours stay in the back of the throat (good oil should not leave a residue in the mouth). So we have intrinsic and extrinsic qualities that we experience through tasting, that we can *only* get from tasting. The intrinsic qualities seem to be in the oil, and the extrinsic qualities seem to be in the mind.

Let's take one more philosophical step backwards. The underlying question that needs to be addressed is whether we can derive *knowledge* from taste, and if so what kind of knowledge that might be. I can say 'this is coffee', or 'this coffee is strong', or even 'this coffee is good'. But the fine taste discriminations are not propositional. What we get from taste is, I suggest, a form of knowledge that is deeply aesthetic in nature, since it is completely derived from the senses, and also deeply dependent on experience. Aesthetic knowledge, then, is the basis of our ability to understand the look, feel, sound and taste of various sensuous objects in the world. We perceive and experience through sense experience, and these experiences all have individual qualia, or experiences of 'what it is like'. For philosophers of mind, this sense of 'what it is like' is called a 'feel'. I smell my morning coffee and it is my experience of the smell of that coffee. I feel rough sandpaper and it is my experience of the sandpaper. Qualia, or feels, or sensations, are not the same as knowledge, however, and their connection to knowledge is tenuous. Since we do not all have the exact same qualitative feels, we might not be able to have the same propositional knowledge. But we do all experience the world primarily through qualia, or these sensations, and from there interpret concepts, metaphors, objects and the external world.

I would argue that gustatory knowledge can be derived from taste. This kind of knowledge is something that taste can provide in a way that no other sense can. Significantly, taste, *separated from touch and smell*, is deeply theoretical. Taste, touch and smell are intertwined so closely that it is important to remember that discussions of each one separately are only theoretical. Taste without smell is virtually impossible, and in order to taste one always senses temperature and texture. Taste is also dependent on the transactional relationship between the inner and the outer, the object and the subject, the external thing and the ingestion of that thing. Our mouths and tongues function not only as receptacles for nutrition and pleasure, but like a radar detector that can distinguish flavours, flavour combinations, textures, spiciness and the most subtle distinctions of flavour. We do not just ingest food but taste it as we transform it. We chew, food mixes with our saliva, and what we swallow eventually gets absorbed into our bodies. We may pay more or less attention to tasting, but the potential is there in most of what we ingest. Taste is the gateway between us and the world outside. The mouth and the sense of taste can act as its own interpretive lens through which we taste not only sweet, sour, bitter, salty and umami, but our mother's cooking and the cuisine of other cultures through their distinctive flavours, and we can learn to differentiate flavours more carefully than we have before. Eating and tasting provide a kind of experience that no other sense can.

A Paradox of Taste

There is a philosophical paradox here as well: the so-called paradox of taste. It rests in the divide between recognizing on the one hand that taste is subjective, and on the other that there are compelling reasons to claim widespread agreement about flavours and distinctions. The philosopher David Hume started us down this path in his essay 'Of the Standard of Taste', and the groundwork he laid has been difficult for us to move away from. Hume claimed that our sentiments, or opinions, can all be right, but that there is only one right judgement. Sentiment is a preference, but judgement is based on reason.[25] Sentiment is internal and personal, but judgement is external and objective. Hume says: 'No sentiment represents what is really in the object. It only marks a certain conformity or relation between the object and the organs or faculties of the mind; and if that conformity did not really exist, the sentiment could never possibly have being.'[26] Although Hume talks almost exclusively about literature in his essay, he does make one comment about gustatory taste, using it only as a metaphor about how absurd it would be to look for beauty or deformity *in* an object. This would be like looking for the *real* sweetness or *real* bitterness, he says.[27] Hume's epistemology assumes that sentiments, sensations and preferences are all subjective, and at the same time he knows that given the right kind of experiences, education, training and refined sense organs, one could ultimately become a 'true judge' and be able to reliably ascertain beauty in any object that had it, despite the fact that beauty, he says, is only in the mind. Thus Hume ends up being an aesthetic realist about taste because he thinks that the aesthetic properties are *in* the aesthetic objects that we contemplate. This is ironic since he is so sceptical about causal realism and is famous for arguing elsewhere that we can have no absolute certainty about matters of causation.

Kant approaches taste with a similar, if not stronger, mistrust. He divides the agreeable and the beautiful in a similar way that Hume divides sentiment and judgement. If something is *beautiful*, it would be beautiful to everyone. If something is *agreeable*, it is only agreeable to me. In other words, I get to have preferences or likes, but to say something is beautiful is to say that it should have universal appeal. Saying that it is 'beautiful to me', Kant says, is nonsensical. He says that if one 'pronounces something is beautiful, then he expects the very same satisfaction of others: he judges not merely for himself, but for everyone, and speaks of beauty *as if it were a property of things*'.[28] For Kant, beauty is a subjective experience of the mind, available for us to experience when we perceive things properly.[29] And he says that because we have similar conceptual frameworks, we should be able to come up with matching assessments of external objects. But food, for Kant, can only be gratifying or agreeable, never beautiful, since beauty must always be apprehended with disinterestedness. And we never take a disinterested approach to our food. Besides, it would be strange to describe my ice cream flavour as beautiful, since I want to eat it only to satisfy my physical desires.

This paradox of taste forces us to decide where beauty is, where pleasure resides and whether or not we can have universal agreement about whether or not something is beautiful. Is beauty in the object? In the subject? How can I be sure about it? Our entire vocabulary of knowledge is built around what we call 'objective knowledge', knowledge of something that is outside of us. We do not even have meaningful terms for knowledge of the bodily senses. But for me, the paradox of taste is not actually about *beauty*, but about *taste* – literal taste and how we are sure of what we are tasting. These are questions that philosophers have struggled with since antiquity, but they really came to the fore in the eighteenth century. The disappointing answer is that it really depends on whose metaphysics and whose epistemology you adopt. For Kant, in order to be able to make claims about pure aesthetic judgement, one must be able to contemplate an object disinterestedly, separate from any instrumental value that the thing might have, but food and drink always have instrumental value, since we need them to survive. For Hume, we can only come to an idealized theoretical standard of taste, given a multitude of proficiencies that are virtually impossible to achieve. Discussions of this abstract view of beauty have flowed generously from the ideas of these two philosophers in the ensuing three hundred years, but the *absolute abstraction* of the notion of taste, I believe, has skewed the discussions of gustatory taste. If the subject–object distinction were collapsed, the paradox of taste would collapse as well. If we start with gustatory knowledge as actually being knowledge, there is no paradox and we do not need to wonder where beauty lies.

Perhaps, then, we need a different model with which to think about taste. I mention Kant and Hume because they are so influential to the way that we have come to think about issues in aesthetics, but I am not sure that their epistemologies are not somewhat outdated in terms of what we now understand about experience and perception – and taste. There is more recent conceptual work about perception, but it still almost always defaults into discussions of vision. I will try to make sense of some of it for taste. We gather all of the knowledge of the world initially through perception. We look at the floor and determine that it is flat, or we look out of the window and determine that it is snowing outside. We taste a grape and determine that it is round and sweet. In order for these kinds of perceptions to become knowledge, they have to be true and we have to have good reasons for believing them. This is one of the mainstays of most forms of epistemology. We know that our senses trick us on occasion (a spoon looks bent in half a glass of water, even though it isn't) but in general our senses provide reliable input for us to navigate around the world, interact very precisely with different objects and smell and taste a huge variety of foods. We call this 'perceiving-as' or, in general parlance, 'seeing-as'. For my purposes, I will call it 'tasting-as'. Our ability to perceive the world is not the same as having certainty that we perceive it correctly. This is the basis of Descartes' scepticism (and desire to prove that we could perceive with certainty). He wanted to demonstrate the link between our perceptions of the world and irrefutable knowledge that we are perceiving the world correctly. We still desire this kind of certainty of perception, even though we don't need to take on the radical scepticism that Descartes did. But taste, just like vision, does not always perceive everything, and what it does perceive is largely dictated by experience and attention. I want to be careful here not to confuse the kind of taste I am talking about (gustatory taste) with taste-as-preference. Gustatory taste dictates a huge number of the experiences we have when interacting with the world around us, so I want to give it sufficient credit for the work it does.

Perhaps the paradox of taste is not actually a paradox – not counter-intuitive or self-contradictory that one might have both objective and subjective experiences simultaneously. It may be the case that we experience this duality more than we think we do. With vision, we think we see objectively for the most part, but we can be encouraged by others to see images in clouds, to identify objects that we did not originally see, or to recognize a building or painting as belonging to some particular style. We also recognize subjective preferences for colour, say, while thinking that we are having an accurate or objective view. Vision offers what I will call relatively *stable* sense experience. Taste, on the other hand, is more fragile. Although we may be tasting a sip from the same bottle of wine, or a slice of the same pie, our perceptions might be very different from those of others. Education, age, smoking or lots of spicy foods can literally change the way we taste different foods. I have already mentioned the genetic variation that makes coriander (cilantro) taste like soap to some people. So-called 'supertasters' have a different genetic variation that makes cruciferous vegetables (especially broccoli and kale) taste more bitter than they do for the rest of the population. Some prescription drugs change the way some foods taste, and people who take these drugs for a long period of time can literally forget what certain foods taste like. In this way it might be said that the sense organ, in this case the tongue, is not in good working order. But since we do not have the same opportunity for objective correction in the way we do with vision, taste ends up being much more fragile in this way. If I do not know that some people taste coriander the way I taste soap, I might think they overreact when I garnish a dish with it. But for them, coriander objectively tastes like soap.

Wittgenstein shed some light on subjectivity when he talked about the possibility of private languages.[30] But languages have grammars, rules and signs that are consistent enough for one person to understand it, and thus it must be possible for others to follow. A private taste experience is not the same as a private language since it is about direct sensory experience. Ironically, language is the vehicle that connects us to others and their taste experiences. Our ability to describe what we taste is the way we know we are having similar subjective experiences as others. However, if our taste vocabulary is limited, we are less capable of connecting on the subtleties of taste and we are left merely with preferences, and claims that 'I like this' and 'I don't like that.' We can do better than that if we cultivate our knowledge of taste, and recognize that the sense of taste is not a sense that can provide knowledge in the same way vision can.

Knowing Food

Gustatory knowledge is different from the kind of knowledge that we get from aesthetic testimony. The contemporary philosophers Aaron Meskin and Jon Robson, for instance, argue that *aesthetic testimony* can provide us with reliable *aesthetic judgements*, or, as they say, it has some 'epistemic value'.[31] They claim that one does not need first-hand experience of something in order to form correct judgements about it in an aesthetic context or in a gustatory one, because having reliable sources *tell* you about the quality of a dish or a restaurant can produce correct beliefs. They qualify their claim a bit by saying that this kind of 'testimony will provide some warrant [or justification] for a *belief* but not warrant sufficient for *knowledge*.'[32] But they then go on to say that aesthetic testimony *can* 'provide strong prima facie motivation for believing that in the right circumstances testimony *can be a source of gustatory knowledge*.'[33] According to Meskin and Robson, the kind of gustatory knowledge we can get is called taste-imony (an ingenious term coined originally in the TV show The Simpsons). Just as we can accept reliable beliefs to make accurate judgements about films and paintings from testimony, they argue that we can also form correct beliefs about food from restaurant reviews, informal recommendations and professional tasters who guarantee quality and consistency. But what they are talking about is the true justified belief kind of knowledge. And on their account, if one has a true belief and the justification comes from a reliable source, then that should count as knowledge. In their view, they take a hard objectivist stance about how we experience taste, and the kind of beliefs that we might have about what we have tasted.

I do not agree with their claim, since I believe that direct experience is required for the kind of gustatory knowledge that

I want to defend. Meskin and Robson suggest that gustatory knowledge is objective, or conceptual – I have a correct idea of the way something tastes – but taste is not about an idea or a belief. Taste is about an experience, and it is about the kind of experience that is direct and immediate but can also be extremely precise (and sometimes not precise at all). The kind of claim I want to make about aesthetic knowledge, or maybe even gustatory knowledge, is that we gain knowledge from tasting that we can get no other way. When we taste, we open ourselves up to the possibilities of both the intrinsic and extrinsic qualities of a particular food. The more experience we have of tasting, the more potential flavours we can experience. The less experience, the less we taste, and the less we know. Without direct experience, we cannot know what a particular oil tastes like.

This dispute evaporates with a bit of clarification about our terms. The philosopher Frank Sibley makes a nice distinction between what he calls particular and generic tastes and smells. He says that 'a generic taste or smell is a sort of classification, within which distinctions can be made, e.g. the taste of honey, and the smell of new-mown hay . . . A particular taste or smell is e.g. the taste of this glass of wine, here, now, at a given temperature.'[34] So, it is like the difference between types and tokens, but with sense experience. Sibley says that anything with a particular taste has the exact same taste as any other thing with the exact same particular taste, but that is not the same situation as with the same generic taste.[35] Generic taste would include Chardonnay, mango or olive oil, but the particulars would be the Wayfarer Vineyard Chardonnay from 2017, the mango I had for breakfast this morning and a Quattrociocchi Olivastro olive oil made from olives from a single farm in the Liguria region of Italy. I believe that Meskin and Robson are talking about generic tastes, and I am talking about particulars. Presumably our ideas of the generic come from multiple instances of the particulars, so there is a connection between the two, but the generic cannot be the self-same as any particular. For me, the particulars can vary so much that the generic is really only theoretical, perhaps in the same way that Platonic forms exist. They are conceptual ideals that bring together all of the particular experiences I have of various tastes and smells. But it is still important that we can connect the particulars to accurate ideas of the generic, and this actually does produce objective knowledge. When I eat a mango it is important that I am able to identify it correctly as a mango and not as a peach. Otherwise I can begin to have false beliefs about which foods are which and my expectations about food begin not only to be wrong-headed, but incredibly disappointing.

Part of the reason I reject Meskin's and Robson's focus on the concept, or idea, of a taste is because this model appeals to a notion of food that is largely standardized. Processed food is created to have the same taste across regions, states and continents. McDonald's, for instance, goes to great lengths to ensure that all of their products taste the same wherever they are sold. Part of the appeal of these kinds of food is the reliability and consistency of taste. Especially while travelling, many people do not want to risk eating something they might not like. This has extended beyond fast food to supermarkets, chain restaurants and global coffee chains. Foods are broken down into component ingredients, mixed with flavour enhancers and stabilizers, enriched with extra ingredients and then put into a form virtually unrecognizable from where it started. Presumably if we 'know' the taste of these foods, then we can have a correct (justified) belief about what they are. This is the generic idea of these things, perhaps, but this has only been possible since the twentieth century with the advent of processed food.

Before the rise of standardized or processed foods (before the advent of the supermarket, microwave dinners and refrigerated transport), people knew better how to differentiate flavours because they were *all* more variable. Olive oil is something that I believe resists standardization since it must be pressed when the olives are ripe and within 24 hours of being picked. Extra virgin olive oil is basically fruit juice, and like any other fruit juice is subject to a huge variety of flavours based on the variety of olive used, the climate it is grown in, how long the olives rested before being pressed, and whether or not the farmer used olives that had fallen to the ground or fresh ones picked from a tree. Furthermore, in Italy at least, wherever you go, they claim to have *the best* olive oil. This regional pride is palpable as the olives vary from north to south, the climate varies from ocean to mountain, and the sun and rain change the flavours of all of the regional oils.

Oil and Fraud

My original claims here were about olive oil and fraud. There are many reasons one might think it important to be able to differentiate good oil from bad, or pure oil from oil cut with cheaper substitutes: health reasons, of course, and wanting to know you are getting what you are paying for. For me, the reason I suggest that one can have a greater appreciation for a good olive oil is because there is literally more there to experience. If we have false beliefs about what olive oil is supposed to be like (maybe that it should not be peppery, or that it should not have a strong taste), then we miss out on an experience of oil that is authentic. We become gullible and thus much more likely to be subjected to fraud. If we do not learn to taste, then it does not matter what we buy or what we eat, since we will not *know* the difference. Without the knowledge gained from a refined ability to taste, we are more susceptible to false beliefs about all kinds of foods, drinks and tastes. If we become easily fooled then we miss out on something important, just as we do with art when we buy a fake thinking we are buying an original.

So what is the account that might resolve the paradox of taste and give meaning to gustatory knowledge? First is the recognition that taste is fundamentally different from vision, and that epistemologically we cannot have the same kind of object–subject distinction. Taste is unmediated by distance, but this does not mean that it cannot have a reflective or cognitive component. We also need to reject the notion that tastes cannot be educated. Exposure and reflection can help to develop a more refined palate, not just for high-end food, but for a range of tastes and qualities that are not readily available to everyone. Hume might call this the delicacy of taste, this ability to make fine distinctions, but he was not referring to gustatory taste in his general theory (ironically, the example he uses to explain this concept *is* about gustatory taste – that of wine). But tasting, the *activity* of tasting, is one that admits of change as one ages, as one is exposed to new and different kinds of foods, drinks and cuisines, develops a clear sense of what one likes and doesn't like, and as one begins to learn to make careful distinctions about *quality* and *taste*.

So if I reject, or put aside, vision-centred propositional knowledge as being my primary goal, and accept that it is possible to learn to make fine distinctions when tasting food and drink, then it is possible to open the gates for another kind of knowledge – gustatory knowledge. With gustatory knowledge, we can discriminate between good and bad, rotten and sweet, lemons and batteries, low quality and high quality. People with gustatory knowledge can differentiate between fusty oil and musty oil, and they can experience the peppery burn of good olive oil as something positive. But having gustatory knowledge is really akin to being able to differentiate colours or sounds. As a musician I have been trained to identify various intervals and so I have a *knowledge* that people with untrained ears do not have. This is not just about hearing or identifying intervals, but also about recognizing counterpoint, parallel fifths, chord progressions and resolutions. I will call this auditory knowledge. This kind of knowledge is not instinctive but must be learned, and it is available to everyone who learns to pay attention in certain ways. But these kinds of knowledge, auditory and gustatory (and visual, and tactile, and olfactory), do not include the *aesthetic* aspect just yet. This is where pleasure needs to be reintroduced. The ability to find pleasure in correct distinctions, resolutions, combinations and expressions of food, drink, music and art more generally is the way we gain access to aesthetic knowledge. So while philosophers have debated for centuries about where beauty lies, in the mind or in an object, this might miss the point of real aesthetic experience, which is in finding pleasure in the sensory impressions of the world around us.

Ironically, if the theory *starts* from gustatory taste, aesthetic knowledge seems intuitive and simple, whereas if we start with a vision-based epistemology it seems counter-intuitive and ripe for rejection since the dependence on distance, both physical and psychological, is built directly into the account. Accounts that build in a subject–object detachment leave no room for the bodily senses and the satisfaction that we can get with bodily experience. Taste is tricky, since its philosophical history is so intertwined with taste as a physiological sense and taste as a metaphor for finding the right kinds of pleasures in various kinds of experiences. If we reject the vision-centred epistemology as being the standard and give gustatory taste a fair playing field we not only have both intellectual and bodily pleasures, but a wide range of sensations detectable by the mouth, from spicy to sweet, from fresh to vinegar and from grubby to grassy. We know what is good, what we like, what is familiar and what the flavours of different regions are, and we know that the ability to make those distinctions allows us to learn about the world in both fundamental and delightful ways.

5

Food Porn and the Power of Images

'Steamy enough?' he asks in a low voice. I am unable to
answer. Tendrils of vapor rise from my naked breasts.
He has cooked me gently but quickly. Kinky as it might
be, I find myself wanting more and more from this kitchen
Adonis. He holds a tiny silver spoon above me, letting fall,
drop by tantalizing drop, a dark, mysterious dipping sauce.
It is the slowest most sensuous thing imaginable. In her
crushed velvet coop my inner goddess fans herself with
both wings.[1]

So reads *Fifty Shades of Chicken*, the steamy parody of *Fifty
Shades of Grey*. This cookbook describes, in deeply sensual
detail, fifty recipes for cooked chicken. The narrator is a female
chicken (Ms. Hen) being prepared, rubbed and basted by a
'rescuer' who is 'wearing [only] jeans and a clean white apron.
He's young and handsome, with a rakish mop of hair. He has
muscled arms and clearly works out. But it is [his] hands that
have [her] mesmerized. They're smooth, pale, perfectly manicured, and beyond competent.'[2] This 'cookbook' reads like soft
porn, but the deeply disturbing part is that the female chicken
delighted in being tied up, sliced, rubbed, pulled, spanked, jerked
around, flame-licked, hog-tied, spread-eagled and whipped. The
chicken, Ms Hen I should say, delights in being manipulated,
cooked and then devoured. Literally. Imagine Patrick Stewart

slowly describing what happens to this chicken as the young, scantily clad chef has his way with her. Well, imagine no more: Mr Stewart narrates the video teaser for this book himself. As *Fifty Shades of Grey* seemed to demonstrate a sexualized and loving version of sexual abuse, this cookbook parody turns that fantasy into a literal guidebook for sexualizing chicken, the most vanilla protein in the fridge. But don't worry if you don't like chicken; there is also *Fifty Shades of Bacon* and *Fifty Shades of Gravy*. A seemingly endless number of cookbooks sensuously describe an array of cooking techniques, with female ingredients asking to be whipped, beaten and tied up.

I am not sure that this is the *first* thing that comes to mind when I think 'food porn', but this category seems to cover a wide range of examples: sexualizing food, adding edibles to pornography and making images of food somehow larger than life as they glisten and gleam and promise all kinds of satisfaction. There is also a strong connection between objectifying our food and sexualizing women through pornography. This happens when the gaze is fixated on objectification and the separation of that object (women or food) from their everyday context. Food porn is everywhere we look in visual culture – magazines, advertisements, cookbooks, food blogs and social media. And as odd as this seems, it is not immediately clear whether this strange habit of ours, of taking pictures of food and looking at images of food, is philosophically interesting or problematic. What I am interested in here is not so much the oddity of posting snapshots of our dinners on Facebook (which still strikes me as really odd), or the interesting meals we eat while engaging in food tourism on Instagram, but what we would really call food pornography, or food porn.

How might the visual pleasures that we get from food porn challenge some of the notions of the ways in which we see women, appetite, pleasure and satiety? Does food porn serve as a replacement for real food? Or are we really just such visual beings that food porn is part of our natural delight in engaging with the world around us? Food porn is part of our visual culture, but the way that images of food create desire negatively impacts the relationship that we have with food. This happens because of the ways that expectation plays into our desires – for food, sex, love – and the mismatch between what we see and the reality of what we experience. Food and sex are connected in important ways because of their deeply embodied nature. What happens when we shift the focus of those physical needs, desires and satisfactions to a visual substitution is something that can diminish the pleasures of real satisfaction. That is, food porn and sex porn change the nature of the relationship we have to food and sex. Chefs say all the time that we eat with our eyes first, then our nose and only then with our mouths. In this chapter I will examine the way we eat with our eyes.

Let's start by clarifying some terms. u.s. Supreme Court Justice Potter Stewart famously said in a 1964 case about obscenity: 'I shall not today attempt further to define the kinds of material I understand to be embraced within that shorthand description ['of pornography'], and perhaps I could never succeed in intelligibly doing so. But *I know it when I see it*.'[3] The 'I know it when I see it' criterion has been an elusive standard for pornography, and to a certain extent obscenity, ever since. Although it has also been used to dismiss some art that politicians do not like, for the most part we know pornography when we see it and it is a regular enough part of our twenty-first-century visual vernacular. We also know food. We talk about it, we eat it, we search for it, we take pictures of it, we cook foods of our cultures, and food is a fundamental part of our identities.

'Food porn' is what happens when the two worlds of pornography and food culture intersect. Strangely enough, they have a few important things in common. First, both pornography and food have been dismissed from being considered serious art because neither can be appreciated with a disinterested stance. In order to be considered 'fine art', a work needs to be able to be considered from a distance, with no practical concern involved. This kind of disinterestedness, or aesthetic interest, allows one to contemplate a work without thinking about any practical interest in it, such as owning it (and potentially making a profit from it), ingesting it or sexually desiring it.[4] Given the primary functions of pornography and food, both have been diminished because our interests are necessarily too involved. Second, pornography and food both appeal to the body and not the mind. As we saw earlier, this alone makes them second-class citizens for philosophers and art historians. Bodies are fickle and desire different things. There is nothing universal about them, and they are certainly not rational or subject to good argument. The mind is the only thing that can make informed decisions about best practices; pornography and food do not appeal in this way. Third, pornography and food exist largely in order to provide us with aesthetic pleasure, and in doing so they appeal to a lower part of us – our appetite (so say some philosophers). At least since Plato, the appetites have been described as that which are impervious to reason, and that part of the body that is desirous of food, sex, power, laziness, alcohol, excess and probably nothing else good for us. Lastly, and perhaps most interesting *and* most controversial, both pornography and food are predominantly associated with women. In pornography, for the most part, women are pictured just as bodies, separated from the complicated lives they lead. Often, individual body parts are highlighted and made to be larger than life. Certainly body parts that are usually out of view are made visible and are brought into focus. Women's sexuality is put on display for the world to examine. In food culture, the domestication of women is shown clearly through women's magazines, the history of advertising and cookbooks. Traditionally, women cook for their families; they do the domestic work of shopping, preparing food and presenting family dinners. Men obviously cook and eat, but the historical association between women and cooking is undeniable. Food porn arguably utilizes this connection between women and food to sexualize and objectify this relationship.

The first instance of the term 'gastro-porn' was in 1977, when Alexander Cockburn of *The Nation* magazine wrote a collective review of thirteen new books about cooking (including, oddly enough, the 'new' u.s. nutrition guidelines published that year). The whole article is delightfully damning, but in describing a dish by Paul Bocuse in his *French Cooking*, Cockburn considered his recipe so over-indulgent, calling for freshwater crayfish and black truffles, that there is 'something unattainable about those pictures of perfect dishes that generate insatiable desire; [they are] pornographic'.[5] Apparently Bocuse was reminded that neither crayfish nor truffles were available in the u.s., and he was encouraged to leave this recipe out for the American version of the cookbook, along with a few others that also had ingredients unavailable in the u.s. However, he insisted that it be left in, because he hoped that 'readers will enjoy [recipes like these], and when traveling in France, recognize these dishes on the menus and be tempted to order them'.[6] Even though Americans would not be able to *cook* these dishes, Bocuse wanted people to know that they were available, somewhere else, just out of reach. In his review, Cockburn notes the 'curious parallels' between manuals on sexual techniques and manuals for cooking food. He explains that 'true gastro-porn heightens the excitement and also the sense of the unattainable by proffering colored photographs of various completed recipes.'[7] For Cockburn, this was as much about the excess and inaccessibility of the dish as it was about the photos, but it was also a clear reference to the indulgent dishes of the French. Having been born and raised in Scotland and England, this was as much an insult to the French for their extravagance as it was a scolding of the Anglo-American taste for simplicity and outright dull food. Ironically it was a reference to the extravagance of French cooking that incited Cockburn to use the term 'gastro-porn'. Yet his reference was not to images, but to unattainable tastes.

Food porn did not get picked up again in any of the literature about food until 1984, when Rosalind Coward wrote a chapter about 'food pornography' in her book *Female Desire*. Both Cockburn and Coward talked about the ways in which cookbooks and magazine advertising had literally become pornographic by how the images portrayed food as highly stylized, glossy and somehow sexualized. But both these examples happened well before the advent of the Internet, which has since provided us with the easy proliferation of endless images of food. The Internet has since given us endless access to images of all kinds, but food porn had its real coming-out in food blogs beginning in the mid-2000s. Bloggers were able to examine ingredients and dishes closely, in terms of both images and detailed description, but it also allowed amateurs to muse about their own weight-loss secrets, best kid-friendly weeknight meals, baking secrets and more. All you had to have was a computer, and all of a sudden you were a published author. Before this deeply democratic platform you needed a book contract, or a cookbook contract, in order to describe any aspects of your food publicly.

Practically, food porn is something that is experienced visually by consumers. With sexual pornography, what should be experienced through touch is experienced instead only through vision and hearing. Amanda Simpson, who calls herself a food pornographer and has written a book about it (*Food Porn Daily: The Cookbook*), gives a functional definition of food porn as being anything that makes her drool. 'Click, drool, repeat,' she says. 'If it does not make me drool then it is not food porn.'[8] For Amanda, food porn is only about the food, not domesticity, table settings or party planning, such as it might be for someone like Martha Stewart. The urban dictionary has a definition of food porn that includes 'close-up images of juicy, delicious food in advertisements'.[9] Really good food porn almost always includes images of juicy, dripping or moist items that reflect the light perfectly. If you google 'food porn', mostly what you get is cheesy chips and pizza – caloric and fat nightmares.

Thi Nguyen and Bekka Williams have suggested recently that a generic use of the word 'porn' has come into the American vernacular that is different from the pornography associated with sexual stimulation. They state that with this 'account, a representation is used as *generic porn* when it is engaged with primarily for the sake of a gratifying reaction, freed from the usual costs and consequences of engaging with the represented content'.[10] Thus the generic use of porn includes things like 'real estate porn', 'baking porn', 'yarn porn' and, of course, 'food porn'. When one looks at these kinds of image on Instagram or Pinterest, one never *really* intends to buy the beautiful apartments, knit the complicated sweaters or cook the beautiful/healthy/indulgent food. As Nguyen and Williams point out, we have no intention of engaging with the content of the representation, but we *use* the representations for immediate gratification.[11] We can look at images, and often scroll through multiple and seemingly endless pictures, merely to stimulate our imaginations. There is also an important consequentialist aspect of this explanation which emphasizes the fact that we do not have to deal with any of the unpleasant consequences of engaging in the real activities we look at images of. No kitchen to clean, no calories to worry about, no houses to buy and maintain. We look at the 'generic porn' images, and gain satisfaction with no commitment and no mess. These images appeal to an aesthetic dimension of food that is not just to do with taste but with the way it looks, and the way we imagine it. We like looking at food, and we like watching people prepare food. Some people even like watching other people eat (there are entire YouTube 'mukbang' videos dedicated to people eating for the viewer's satisfaction). It seems we sometimes like watching others do these things more than we like doing them ourselves.

But food porn, I think, is different from this generic sense that Nguyen and Williams describe. There is something very sensual about food, and there is a connection between sex and food that just does not exist between sex and real estate, or sex and yarn. Both food and sex can grant us a form of satiety, there is a possibility of excess for both, and both are clearly pleasures that are primarily physical in nature rather than intellectual. Food and sex are both things that we have deep desires for and very specific preferences about. Both are deeply personal. They are the two most important aspects of human survival and are considered two of our most fundamental needs. If this is true, then the relationship we have with images of food might strike us as something much more fundamental than just being visual gluttons, or food voyeurs.

As noted earlier, we are extremely visual beings, and certainly we love looking at all kinds of things. In the early twentieth century

Sigmund Freud introduced us to the notion of scopophilia, which literally means the love of looking. For Freud, the pleasure we take in looking was connected to the idea that life was built around the dual nature of tension and release. Sexual energy created the tension and sexual activity allowed for the release. Merely looking helps to build the tension. In 1975 Laura Mulvey borrowed the concept of scopophilia and used it to explain the ways in which the modern film industry was taking advantage of our love of looking, and reinforcing gendered standards of the lookers and the looked at: men and women respectively. Mulvey coined the term 'male gaze' as defining the way in which men held power over women in three distinct ways: the man behind the camera; the male characters represented as the lookers within narrative film; and the male perspective being the dominant viewer of film.[12] According to Mulvey, and many scholars after her, this way of looking has become dominant within Western society (and possibly elsewhere, too). It is so ingrained in us that few bother to question it or are even aware of it. But this particular way of viewing the world takes on a heterosexual, male perspective where women are typically seen as objectified, passive, servile and always available. In some pornography, they are seen as helpless, needing a man, often not much more than body parts. Women can adopt this male gaze, too, and often do. Women are often the most critical of other women's looks, thereby objectifying other women. Men, in narrative cinema and according to Mulvey's account of the male gaze, are construed as active agents who have the power to make happen whatever they will, and always have the power to look at women.[13]

This objectifying gaze is what has made food porn possible. When we learn that objectifying gaze and then adopt that gaze everywhere, this way of looking begins to dominate how we see in other ways too. This is what has made possible the extreme objectification of food: without this dominant way of looking at the world we might not have adopted this stance about inanimate objects.

Food porn needs to be distinguished from lesser-quality snapshots of food. Just as snapshots of nude people do not necessarily qualify as pornography, neither do low-quality photos of food. Food porn appeals to a set of aesthetic ideals that emphasize the most sensual aspects of food, echoing aspects of human sexuality: phallic imagery of bananas and cucumbers, the round curvature of chicken breasts, aubergines and yonic foods that resemble vaginal openings, such as avocado halves, half-figs, half-oranges and oysters. Of course, some food porn is more like food and some is more like pornography. What might be called a pornographic gaze, sociologist Erin McDonnell explains, is where the 'photographic composition interpolates the camera operator, allowing the photographer to shape the audiences' experience of the food'.[14] Typical of food porn are various different photographic techniques explicitly borrowed from pornography. McDonnell suggests that there are a number of characteristic features of food porn, like extreme close-ups, which impose 'an uncomfortable intimacy conveyed through close proximity to the food object'.[15] A viewer can see details of the object that could normally not be seen at a socially acceptable distance, or even without the use of a close-up lens. With still-image pornography, flaws can be edited out, and this also works for food porn, but with food one can often see detail such as drips or crevices that one would never be able to see with the naked eye. The framing of food porn is very different to snapshots of one's dinner. Food porn tends to include only the food in a photo and rarely a place setting or other distracting objects. The purpose is to focus solely on the food at hand.

McDonnell points out that in the early cookbooks of mid-century America, say, of the Betty Crocker ilk, photographs were taken from arm's length, or showed the view of a dinner, place setting included, so one could imagine it on one's own table. Orientation is another subtle but important aspect of food porn. Lighting, angles and composition all vary, but with food porn, all indications are that there is something beautiful, something sensual and maybe something hidden in whatever is being pictured. It is never utilitarian or merely functional, but sensuous, something that pulls you close so that your senses are titillated. The last feature McDonnell points out is the depth of field, which is a photographic technique that allows focus on only certain parts of an object while blurring others. With food porn, crisped edges, colourful sheens, perfect drips and so on can all be the centre of focus, so that the photography itself can help the viewer's eye know exactly where to go in the visual field.

Photographic techniques, a pornographic gaze, phallic and yonic foods and that which is slightly (or drastically) out of reach for an average person are all typical of food porn and pornography. We have created an entire genre of images that are visual substitutions for that which we should see, smell and taste. Of course much in the history of painting involves representations of objects that are known through first-hand experience, but this exploding genre of food porn has really taken on a life of its own and goes well beyond what has been done in art. In one way, it enters the realm of substitution for actual cooking (since it is estimated that people spend more time watching cooking shows than they do cooking), and in a different way many people are using food porn to develop an extended identity through food-porn tourism as a form of social status.

Porn as Food, Women as Food

One of the ways in which we use food porn is as a replacement for food. It cannot be a literal replacement, of course, but a metaphorical one. This works in the same way that pornography works as a metaphorical replacement for sex. In both cases, however, it is not a very healthy substitution. What is being replaced is important, meaningful and life-giving; what is replacing it is a mere simulation of what one needs. Women have a different kind of relationship with food porn to men, since they have a very different relationship with food. Men have historically been given the better choice of meats, more protein, larger portions; historically, they eat before the women, and they have come to associate themselves closely with meat. Masculinity itself often includes attitudes about meat-eating and consumption that women rarely share – namely that men *need* meat, and that men who do not eat meat are unmasculine or, even worse, feminine.[16] Women, on the other hand, have long felt the need to control their bodies through diet, and tend to eat more vegetables and get less of the meat protein available. Women also tend to worry more about their weight than do men, at least in the last fifty to seventy years when food has become much more widely available in the developed world, bringing an over-surplus of available calories. Some anorexic women look at pictures of food to replace eating. 'Pro-ana' (pro-anorexia) websites suggest that looking at food porn is an effective way to curb hunger and the desire to eat.[17] But more than this, women look at pictures of other women to gauge themselves, and they look at pictures of food to gauge the ideal way they should cook *and* look. In both cases, they end up holding themselves and their skills up to an impossible standard that has been airbrushed, primped and created by a team of experts. When the ideal images replace what is actually possible for women's bodies, the meals they serve or just the way food is supposed to look, body dysmorphia can set in, and nothing will ever quite measure up.

Rosalind Coward, in her book *Female Desire*, paints a picture of the ways in which women desire food, and they desire to eat that which they are not allowed to have. Coward's claims about food porn concern the ways in which it is a real form of fantasy for women. She claims that in the same way men fantasize about women, women fantasize about eating. And just as with sexual pornography, the object of desire is taken completely out of context, devoid of complications and consequences. Women in sexual pornography are objectified in that they are captured in a single instance in time, with nothing but their sexual allure. They are one-dimensional, with no past and no future, no personality and no problems. The same works for food porn. The food is cooked perfectly and is displayed flawlessly on a beautiful table setting. There are no dishes to clean from the making or the eating. A dish with no baggage. For Coward, the images are not just pornographic because they are sexualized images of food, but because the 'glossy, sensual photography legitimates oral desires and pleasures for women in a way that sexual interest for women is never legitimated.'[18] The images can also create a direct connection between food and fat, which quickly moves to pleasure and guilt. The images are all she can have. So much guilt has been associated with gustatory indulgence for women that it is hard to feel the full pleasures of eating any more. So looking at pictures is a (feeble) substitute for real indulgence in sweet, fatty, filling foods. According to Coward, 'sexual pornography is a display of images which confirm men's sense of themselves as having power over women, [and] food pornography is a regime of pleasurable images which has the opposite effect on its viewers – women.'[19] Men imagine themselves dominating women sexually with pornography but women can only imagine themselves indulging in the pleasures of eating the rich, indulgent foods that are represented in photos.

The idea that women are only allowed to indulge in photos, not real food, is still deeply enforced today with websites and blogs with names like 'hungry girl' and 'eat me guilt free', both sites for recipes. As far as I can tell, most advertisements directed at women are about reducing the amount of food they eat and getting a better body. It is not just that thin is an ideal, but fat is unlovable and out of control. In one study, it was shown clearly that people who eat a healthy diet and who are thin are perceived as more moral, more intelligent and more attractive.[20] Unfortunately the converse is true as well, and people who eat high-fat, high-carb diets and who are considered overweight are considered less moral, less intelligent and less attractive. An advertisement by marketing company MO4 depicts a woman with cake around her mouth, holding a picture of a whole cake, standing in front of a height strip as though she is in a mug shot. She is clearly guilty, given her horrified expression and the cake on her shirt. The strip behind her is not measuring her height, however, but her weight, ringing in at an astonishing 80 kg (176 lb). Her weight makes her guilty, and her cake makes her guilty. The advertisement is for 'guiltfree foods' – healthy foods that one never has to feel bad about eating.[21] These kinds of ads are insidious and ubiquitous. They teach both women and men that food can be good and bad, that there are good calories and bad calories and, worst of all, eating can make you bad – and guilty. And when we are guilty, we need to be punished, in this case most likely either by starvation or at the gym. If we indulge only in the photos, then maybe we will not be so guilty (maybe that chicken wants to be punished for being bad, too!).

According to Coward, women like to look at images of food and to read cookbooks in bed so that they can simulate eating. They fantasize about eating that which is forbidden. They fantasize about that which can only produce guilt and shame. But when women abstain from food, they also abstain from desire in an attempt to control aspects of their being that do not need to be controlled except in ways that social circumstances might dictate. Coward even adds that most women she knows read cookbooks in bed. She says, 'Few activities it seems rival relaxing in bed with a good recipe book.'[22] She notes that women use 'recipe books as aids to oral gratification, stimulants to imagine new combinations of food, ideas for producing a lovely meal.'[23] According to Coward, women fantasize about eating, and also like to imagine how they will prepare tasty meals for their husbands and families. Coward's claim seems to suggest the opposite of what *Fifty Shades of Chicken* portrays. In *Fifty Shades* (of chicken *or* bacon), the female is portrayed as *wanting* to be handled, constrained and consumed. This is a much more male-centred approach to pornography, however. As Coward argues, men often use pornography to imagine dominating and consuming women. Women use food porn to dominate their own appetite for eating.

Although I have never read a cookbook in bed, it seems unfortunate to me that this would be something that adult women might do instead of eating. But just as pornography is something that people can use instead of sex, what looking at images of food can do is something vicarious and different from engaging in any real activity. In reality, no one's food looks like it does in food porn. It is not glossy or dripping in just the right way. No real food can stand the close-ups. But this is what food porn can give us that real food cannot. It idealizes the food and objectifies it, just as pornography objectifies bodies. Food porn elevates ordinary food to an aesthetic object that can be considered alone, visually.

Historian Rachel Cleves suggests that women's tendency to want to look at food instead of eating it has a long history. One of the roots of this history comes from the early Methodist tradition and its founder John Wesley. His recommendations for a diet in his book *Primitive Physic* included mostly bland foods containing no spices. He suggested that 'nothing conduces more to health than [sexual] abstinence and plain food.'[24] With his proclamation that 'all pickled, or smoked, or salted food, and all high-seasoned, is unwholesome,' Wesley made a clear connection between seasoned food and immorality. Cleves writes about several women who were raised in cultures that advocated Wesley's strictures about food. Elizabeth David, a cookbook author from the twentieth century, is said to have actively set aside all of Wesley's imperatives when she 'feverishly wrote out recipes calling for apricots, olives and butter, rice and lemons, oil and almonds.'[25] David is also noted for saying, 'I came to realize that in the England of 1947, those were dirty words that I was putting down,' since 'such open expressions of pleasure in eating were considered taboo.'[26] Women were reading about indulgent foods and looking at pictures in cookbooks even when they were a clear indication of moral instability, as gluttony and lust have been two sides of the same coin since early Christianity. One was said to lead directly to the other. Cleves notes that the fourth-century Christian monk Evagrius of Pontus declared that gluttony was the mother of lust and that 'the pleasures of taste led directly to sexual desire.'[27] Given the prohibitions against sexual desire, especially for women, reading about food and looking at pictures have long been a welcome substitute for actual debauchery.

Harvey Kellogg advocated a similar kind of diet as Wesley in the early twentieth century at his sanatorium in Battle Creek, Michigan. Kellogg (who invented corn flakes as part of this high-carb, all-vegetarian diet) advocated strict sexual abstinence, excessive chewing (or 'fletcherizing') and daily yoghurt enemas. He believed that the bacteria in yoghurt could help to clear out the colon. This would thoroughly cleanse both the body and the mind so that one could remain moral and healthy, which were seen to be one and the same by Kellogg. He warned against meat, alcohol and spicy foods and claimed that they would all stimulate sexual urges and weaken the body, making it prone to disease. Kellogg initially followed Seventh Day Adventist teachings about food and sex, where he developed anaphrodisiac foods (said to reduce libido) and was an early advocate of the 'clean living movement', which helped to make reforms against alcohol and tobacco. Ironically Kellogg was 'disfellowed' from the Church, but he believed in the teachings and continued to preach against meat, spice, alcohol, sex and masturbation. According to Kellogg, the two sexes did not need to be dealt with differently, but restraint and denial were both held in the highest esteem by this early diet and wellness entrepreneur.[28] This is one of the kernels of the attitude that has developed which favours guilt over pleasure and *looking* a particular way over being content with bodies that work, age, sag and, most importantly, get hungry and desirous.

The link between guilt and eating is extremely powerful. And, importantly, pleasure seems to be the common denominator between the shame of eating and the shame of sexual desire. If women are given the message that the images all around them are what they are supposed to aspire to, then doing things that they know will not help to create that image, the minimum they end up with is cognitive dissonance, and worse, guilt, confusion and an unhappy and unhealthy relationship with food. Looking at food porn can help alleviate the negative feelings that have come to be associated with the sinful nature of eating too much, or even deriving pleasure from what one eats.

The Art of Food

A picture may be worth a thousand words, but it is not very filling. Food porn obviously does not fill our bellies, but it does satisfy us in some other ways. In just the way that pornography fills some kind of need or desire, representational images of food seem to do the same. Of course there are as many kinds of pornographies as there are tastes of people who consume them, but having images stand in for real experiences is nothing new to humans. The early uses of food porn have morphed into something much more common, and mundane, with the advent of the television and now the Internet. We have been taken with television fantasies for some time now, at least since the 1950s, when televisions became overwhelmingly popular and made their way into most u.s. households. But there is something radically passive about our consumption of food porn on tv, when we watch others cook and eat while imagining doing it ourselves.

Representations of food, however, came much earlier than television and magazine advertisements. The history of art is filled with examples of paintings of food. Not just the notorious still-life of a bowl of fruit, but paintings of people eating, feasts, luscious textures of fruits, breads and meats abound. In the seventeenth century, Dutch still-life painting was elevated to an important form as more and more people had access to paints and training, and it became more common to have paintings in middle-class homes. This genre of painting was not just about the difficult techniques of getting the textures and perspectives of fruit and bread right: the paintings also gave indications of wealth and status, and of access to produce, meat and fish. These paintings would end up having an impact on Western painting for the next two hundred years because food painting was held in such high esteem. As was typical of this era, arrays of food laid out on a table would not be perfectly arranged, but rather set in such a way that indicated that an eater had just been there moments before. This invites the viewer to be a part of the food that is laid out.

In a painting by Pieter Claesz., *Still-life with Lobster and Crab*, the food on the table is in disarray, not neatly or symmetrically ordered as it would be at a proper table. An orange is partially peeled, the bread is broken, ready to eat, and the knife is left on the table as if it had just been set down, with the handle available for the viewer to pick up. The peeled orange invites the viewer to imagine its smell. The cracked bread invites the viewer to anticipate its taste. One of the most striking aspects of many of these seventeenth-century paintings is the way the painting engages the viewer, making them part of the painting. As art historian Kenneth Bendiner explains, 'the viewer is the diner, hence all those knives with their handles directed outwards – they are invitations to join the meal.'[29]

This is not unlike many of the paintings of the twentieth century by Picasso, for instance his *Les Demoiselles d'Avignon*, an abstract painting of a group of prostitutes in Barcelona. This is a painting of five (not incidentally nude) women who are all facing forward in a ring; at the front of the ring is supposed to be the viewer. Interestingly, there is also a piece of melon in the foreground, perhaps reminiscent of a still-life of fruit, but the melon, along with the women, has been given sharp angles and intimidating edges which are not at all reminiscent of luscious fruit or inviting women. The sketches for the painting had included a foregrounded figure whose back would be to the viewer so that the circle of women was complete in the painting, but with that figure missing in the final painting, there is a clear invitation to the viewer to imagine themselves as involved. This is the same kind of invitation that the food still-lifes from the seventeenth century started us off with: to be participants in the image, rather than an outside observer who can contemplate objectively what is going on in the painting. It is not incidental that paintings of nudes and paintings of food both end up being inviting in the same way. When the perspective of paintings are made in this way, the viewer is supposed to feel more included, since they are really standing just at the fourth wall. While some paintings clearly position the viewer as an outside observer, in others the placement of cutlery, plates and food are positioned for easy access, inviting the viewer into the pictorial space.

The ideal of objectivity is also one of the important aspects of aesthetic disinterestedness. The lower senses (taste, smell and touch) do not offer the proper distance. As the early twentieth-century philosopher Edward Bullough says, 'psychical distance' does not allow one to objectively contemplate what is perceived. As Bullough explains, 'the actual spatial distance separating objects of sight and hearing from the subject has contributed strongly to the development of the monopoly' of sight dominating aesthetic pleasure.[30] But these kinds of paintings reject that approach, as does much pornography, I presume, which invites the viewer to imaginatively engage with the subject, not distance themselves. So even though painting and pornography are both visual, they both invite the viewer to collapse the distance between viewer and viewed. Presumably this is one of the primary distinctions between art and pornography: objectivity. The same images can function as art when viewed disinterestedly, and when viewed 'with interest' are interpreted as pornography. The contemporary philosopher Hans Maes rejects the argument that pornography and art are mutually exclusive on the basis that, with a single representation, we might have different kinds of reactions. Most scholars, he says, reject pornography because of the lack of aesthetic and artistic quality, but he argues that in the end there are no *inherent* differences. Future pornographers, though, should heed the call to better, more interesting representations.[31] Food porn need not worry about having itself taken more seriously, as Maes suggests, but as with pornography, its influence is felt not because of its seriousness or importance, but because of its prevalence.

An interesting study was done in 2016 when a group of researchers from the Cornell Food and Brand Lab tried to discover the origins of food porn. They realized that people have been painting food for well over five hundred years. For their study, they narrowed down the five most artistically proficient countries in the West (the Netherlands, France, Italy, Germany and the United States), and assessed paintings that included food and were painted between the years 1500 to 2000. The results were somewhat surprising, although not to any twenty-first-century food blogger: paintings of food did not depict typical meals of the respective households of those who commissioned the works. When paintings were commissioned, people wanted food depicted that was rarer and more upper-class than they typically ate. For instance, most bread in nineteenth-century Europe was made of brown and very coarse bran flour. Only the upper classes ate the finely ground white wheat that tends to be depicted in paintings. Furthermore, although chicken and quail were the most readily available proteins in central Europe, fish and shellfish were painted much more frequently than poultry. In terms of vegetables and fruits, artichokes and lemons were painted the most, but both were relatively rare. Consumer behaviour expert Brian Wansink writes: 'It is understandable that *Dutch* paintings featured large amounts of seafood, because more than 50% of the border of the Netherlands is surrounded by water, and the majority of its population lives within 100 km of the sea, but for Germany – a country that has much more limited access to water – it is notable that 30% of its paintings still feature seafood.'[32] As for the choices regarding fruits and vegetables, the study indicates that some fruits and vegetables might have been chosen not only for status, but because they are more challenging to paint. One surprising generalization found in the study is that the most frequently *depicted* foods are not frequently *eaten* foods. What is not surprising is that there is a disconnect between reality and image, just as there is today.

We are a society filled with images – so many that on most days we do not even realize how many we have seen. Forbes' marketing division estimates that Americans see about four thousand images each day, on television, billboards and of course on our phones and social media.[33] We can barely go outside our homes without being exposed to images selling endless goods and consumer products. The images food porn produce are seemingly innocuous, but in reality they build a background for the beliefs that we have about the way food should look, and the way we think about eating. Images build beliefs, and beliefs construct world views.

Philosophers on Pictures

Ancient worries about representation began with Plato, whose metaphysics included a separation of the 'Forms', or abstract ideals (like beauty), physical manifestations (like a beautiful man), and then reproductions or imitations of the physical manifestations (like a sculpture of a beautiful man). In the *Republic*, as he develops his metaphysics, his main worry at the end of Book 10 is about the quality of education for the children of the ideal city. If one learns from imitations, rather than from the real, then what gets conveyed is not truth, but only a pale reflection of truth. It would be like learning about food from poor photographs of food, or two-dimensional paintings, rather than from a full understanding of what the food is, where it came from, what it is used for and, of course, what it tastes like. If learners believe that they are learning truth while really only learning from imitations, they do not even know to ask for something better, fuller or more real. Plato claims that the lower rungs of imitative knowledge will have a poisonous effect on a person and the only 'antidote' is real knowledge. The imitative arts seem to corrupt 'the mind of all listeners who do not possess as an antidote a knowledge of its real nature'.[34] If you are not taught to value the real, then what you are accustomed to believe is only inconsistently true, and there is no reliable way to discern the difference between truth and mere opinion. So for Plato, there is a central distinction and distance between the real and what is only imitated.

Unfortunately this means that Plato has been interpreted as being an adversary to the imitative arts, including poetry, painting and music. Nowadays this would also include photography, novels (all fiction, really), films and likely most dance. Whatever his intentions, and whatever he said in the *Republic* as being still relevant, he was wary about representations because they focused attention on aspects of an object that were only surface-deep, so to speak, and did not hold the real essence of a thing.

These worries are exactly the worries I have about food porn. It is just a representation of something that we are not really supposed *just* to look at. We are supposed to ingest and taste it. Plato's worries were not merely about understanding a three-dimensional object as a two-dimensional object. They concerned thinking (mistakenly) that one could gain *knowledge* from that two-dimensional object *as if* it were knowledge of the three-dimensional one. With food porn, assuming that we are talking only about the visual kind (and not having Patrick Stewart describing sexy chicken massage to you), the images in food advertisements, say, are made up, just as a model is made up before a photo shoot. In the U.S. food advertising laws require that the actual food that is being advertised is used, but there are professional 'food stylists' whose job it is to make the food look as appetizing as possible. This is done with silicone sprays for shine, stabilizers for ice cream so it does not melt, glue in place of milk for cereal ads (since they are not selling the milk!) so that the cereal appears only on top of the milk, with full texture, and cardboard props between layers of hamburgers to give them extra height. Of course, much food porn is also created by skilled chefs, not what the Food Network has come to call mere 'home cooks'.

What we see in advertisements is not what we get on our plates. This is evidenced by any fast food hamburger, cereal, cheesy pizza or cake that glistens in pictures but pales by comparison in reality. The problem, according to Plato, is not about knowledge but about belief, and if one has faulty *beliefs* about the world, it is impossible to have reliable *knowledge*. One of the problems with food porn is that it provides us with faulty information about the world and we are bound to be disappointed when we get the real thing. Worse than being disappointed, we are more likely also to be wrong.

In his 'Simulacra and Simulation' (1981), Jean Baudrillard addressed the problem that Plato alerted us to, but with a very modern approach.[35] Baudrillard recounts one of Jorge Luis Borges's famous fables about the cartographers of an empire who have been called to make a detailed map of a territory. The cartographers make the map so big and so detailed that it covers the entire land. As the empire eventually crumbles, so does the map, and the frayed map ends up being an accurate metaphor for the decaying empire. Ironically, the 'ageing double' is ultimately confused with the real thing.[36] This is what Baudrillard calls the 'finest allegory' of simulation, where the replica ends up having more meaning and reality than the original. It is an allegory where 'simulation is no longer that of a territory, a referential being or a substance. It is the generation by *models of a real without origin or reality*: a hyperreal.'[37] What he means is that the country no longer provides a model for the map, but rather the map defines the country. The map becomes *more real* than the country and the country ceases to exist. The relationship between the map and the land is not one of representation, but of appearance, and that appearance becomes reality. Ultimately the original disappears completely and all we are left with is the imitation, or simulation. There is no original for Baudrillard, but only a copy; the copy is real in the sense that it is a new standard, and a new basis for opinion and knowledge.

As we look endlessly at highly stylized images, we forget that they do not resemble or represent the original. And it is in that forgetting that new meanings are constructed. The McDonald's hamburger we buy never resembles the one in the advertisements, but the advertisements become reality to the viewers, and it is what we think of when we think about those burgers. Baudrillard's hyperreality seems counter-intuitive, since most of us seem quite capable of distinguishing the real from the representational. But as potentially devastating as his account might have been in the early 1980s, it has predicted a very accurate reality for us in the twenty-first century. The hyperreal is where reality and fiction are seamlessly intertwined to an extent that one cannot really tell them apart. Reality TV, CGI films, cosmetic surgery, filters on smartphones, airbrushed and Photoshopped images, highly manicured gardens that present nature as tamed, and even professional sports where athletes perform superhuman feats are all examples of the way that the hyperreal is seamlessly blended with the real. Our phones seem to provide a never-ending supply of experiences that recreate reality for us in a variety of ways. For example, I have noticed recently that I am much more likely to look at my phone app to see what the weather is like than to look (or go!) outside. An area that might have more of an impact on creating hyperreality than any other is social media. Here we are able to present a 'reality' of ourselves to our 'friends' which we control completely – only the best photos, only our most interesting versions of experiences and only our best parenting moments. What we see on social media is hardly an accurate presentation of ourselves, but how could it be? Collectively, we invest a huge amount of time and interest in our social media and, for many, the number of 'likes' any given post gets can have a big impact on self-worth, for good or for ill. We can also be susceptible to being 'catfished' by scammers pretending to be someone they are not. The whole nature of the Internet allows for exaggerations, lies, fabrications and half-truths to become what we focus on visually, and ultimately what we take to know as real. What we know and what we think we know become so melded, we can't tell them apart.

A number of films have used this postmodern condition as their backdrop storylines: *The Matrix, Existenz* and *The Truman Show* are just three examples. Although Plato might have predicted something like this failure to distinguish reality from hyperreality, I am sure this would be his worst nightmare: a world where reality and fantasies about reality move seamlessly back and forth between one another. The ability to *know* anything in this world rapidly evaporates. I suppose this is how we get fake news. But this is also a world in which food porn abounds, where images are 'more real' than actual food, and the actual food is in reality not that appealing. This is how we end up with witnesses of mass shootings (or experiences of war) saying, 'It was like a movie.' Their only meaningful reference to a bloodbath like the one they are in the middle of is film.

In *The Matrix* (dir. Lana and Lilly Wachowski, 1999), those who live in the Matrix actually exist in a drab underworld. They know that this is the 'real reality', as they have the true knowledge of what reality is like, while the rest of us inhabit a computer-generated world programmed to produce (false) pleasure. When they eat breakfast, those in the Matrix have a bowl of protein mush, which one character describes as 'a single-celled protein combined with aminos, vitamins, and minerals. Everything the body needs.' But it looks and tastes completely bland. The 'steak scene' is one of the more poignant parts of the film, where Cypher delights in a 'juicy and delicious' steak that he admits is just a sensation created by the Matrix that makes him experience this 'steak'. But he delights in it thoroughly nevertheless. As a reward for helping Agent Smith take down Morpheus, he demands to be returned to the Matrix and to have all memories of the real world erased – especially the knowledge that the juicy steak is a mere sensory simulation. This particular movie has served as a classic philosophical challenge to the question of whether or not we can really know reality. It even includes a nice gesture to Baudrillard at the beginning: in a scan of Neo's apartment, Baudrillard's *Simulacra and Simulation* sits on a table next to the sofa. It is easy to dismiss this radical version of the ways in which we might or might not know reality, but what it does, and what Baudrillard's notion of hyperreality does, is pose exactly the problem that food porn presents. When we interact with a simulacrum of an object, we begin to have a different relationship with that object from the one we can have with the 'real' object. Images begin to influence our expectations.

Baudrillard highlights Disneyland as one of the prime examples of the way we have lost our original empire and valorised the imitation. He says that here the fantasy of *realistic fantasy*, life-size houses from the past (along with an ethos from the past), Chinatown, its own currency, and the special effects created all lend to a false reality, or a hyperreality that does not represent anything real; in philosophical terms, it does not refer properly. People who go to Disney's Chinatown (or Italy, Mexico or to any of the other nation simulations they have) are led to believe they know what it is like to *be* in those places. Baudrillard worries that those Disneyesque experiences will lead people to believe they know what it is like to experience those places without travelling, without understanding another culture or language and without experiencing the whole of a community (even the bad or dangerous parts). Those experiences can replace the experiences of being in the actual places. Chinatown, for example, also serves 'authentic Chinese food' in at least three different restaurants. Like most Chinese restaurants in the West, they serve an Americanized version of Chinese food. 'Authentic' Chinese food is unlikely to be anything Westerners would eat because it includes too many unfamiliar ingredients, as well as fish and other animals that are much fresher (perhaps only partially dead) than we are used to. But we can walk away thinking that we know what Chinese food is like, and perhaps what it is like to be in China. (It includes a replica of the Terracotta Army and a section of the Great Wall.)

On a recent episode of *Top Chef*, where chef-contestants engage in different cooking challenges each week to be crowned Top Chef, one of the challenges included making an 'Instagram-mable' dish (which included various junk foods such as Oreos and Easy Cheese). Whichever dish got the most votes on Instagram would win the challenge. The way food looks, and how good it looks using a smartphone camera, is becoming important in the restaurant industry. People take snapshots of their food (what I might call camera cuisine rather than food porn proper) and geotag their meals in restaurants so that anyone looking at Google Maps will see a snapshot of a meal rather than anything the restaurant itself wants to put on its webpage. The *Top Chef* competition is really putting itself in the growing tradition of creating camera-ready food. Some restaurants have changed their menus because what they have been making does not photograph well; they create new dishes that are often more colourful and more varied on the plate. When chefs develop dishes that make for better photographs, taste takes second place to image. The 'Insta' becomes the real, and the food ceases to exist.

In her article 'How Instagram has Ruined Restaurants', Olivia Petter asks, 'If you didn't Instagram it did it even happen?'[38] Presumably this is a reference to David Hume's query about a tree falling in a forest: does it make a noise if no one's around to hear it? But Instagramming food (and all other aspects of one's life) has become so prevalent today that it is a joke that everyone understands. Reasons for this vary from socio-economic explanations to do with showing off the kinds of foods one eats, to one's health habits, to one's cooking/baking skills, to straight-up social status. And although we do tend to Instagram much of our lived experiences (*especially* what we buy), part of what may be going on is that we want to share our meals with others. Sharing meals reflects a very basic human instinct, and has been an important part of family, friendship, religion and culture for millennia. Instagramming meals may be performative, but according to Petter, it is also an invitation, 'extending, basically, the number of people at one's table'.[39]

Whether it is sexy chicken or an overindulgent brownie dripping with caramel sauce, food porn brings to the foreground the visual, and often sexual, nature of our food. It also brings to the foreground the *sensual* nature of food, and the ways in which we attempt to capture a moment or a meal. Although there are no strict boundaries around what counts as food porn, its similarities to sexual porn allow it to be elevated to show that cooking and eating can express deep levels of excess, delight and desire. Just eating does not allow food to be elevated in the same way, since it is not shared beyond one's own table. Whether an attempt to let others know that we can cook, that what we eat is interesting, delicious or indulgent, or that we are experimenting with new cuisines on our travels, food porn allows us to capture in time something that we have never captured before – the *image* of food.

6

On Recipes and Rule Following

'Culture, when it comes to food,' writes American food writer
Michael Pollan, 'is of course, just a fancy word for your
mom.'[1] The Italian food historian Massimo Montanari goes even
further – for him, 'food *is* culture.'[2] Food exemplifies culture
when it is produced, when it is eaten and when we choose some
foods over others. Montanari's and Pollan's claims both indicate
how deep the connection is between who we are, the ways we
think about ourselves and how we do this through eating and
cooking. But what really allows these two claims about food and
culture to be true is the transformative nature of cooking itself.
When we cook – whether we are 'moms' or not – we change what
is nature and turn it into culture. We take what is available to
us according to where we live in order to feed our families. We
create meals that are not only nutritious but embed meaning
with ethnic and religious significance into families and communities. We transform the raw ingredients into the cooked dishes
that take on new flavours, textures and qualities so that we can
digest them more easily, but also so that we can enjoy a wide
variety of food more fully.

Philosophically speaking, this means that cooking is central
to issues of identity (what does the food I eat say about who I
am?), as well as absolutely foundational to the ways in which
we think of what is real and meaningful, and understand how
we approach different modes of inquiry. The nature of cooking

exemplifies the nature of change as it transforms nature into culture. Changing food into culture is the basis of many religious practices, cultural and national identity, and eating together is one of the primary ways in which we connect with others. Eating well is one of the most important aspects of being able to live a good life, but I want to examine not just what it means to eat well, but how *cooking* can provide a platform for making sense of philosophical theories and frameworks. Knowing *how* to cook is not instinctual, however, and how we learn to cook and how we account for that knowledge is important.

People have to cook to survive but this practice has not been given much credit or scrutiny in the history of philosophy, given that eating well has so much to do with living well. I believe that cooking has not been taken seriously by philosophers because it is typically something that women have done the bulk of for much of human history. The ways in which cooking can be used as a model for thinking through problems is one that we have never really seen, because examples are normally taken from the typical activities of men.[3] Food is transient, since it is in the nature of food to be cooked and ingested, not to be contemplated for generations, as paintings are. Cooking is practical, not theoretical. And eating is, of course, deeply associated with the physical nature of the body. This is something else philosophers tend to downplay, since the subjective nature of physical existence is so incredibly difficult to characterize, especially in comparison to the workings of the mind.

Are there more fruitful ways in which cooking can be used as a model of philosophical theory-making? Could cooking be used as a third option for some of the dichotomies that we end up roping ourselves into, that involve the way we tend to think about theory and practice? Thinking about cooking, in other words, might tell us more than just what is for dinner. It can help us to think about problem-solving in a whole new way.

Cookery Begins and Ends with Plato

Philosophers talk about the senses, taste and the role of food in good and fair government, but there is only one well-known reference to the physical act of cooking. In Plato's dialogue *Gorgias* (which ironically takes place during a dinner party), Socrates compares rhetoric to 'cookery' in an attempt to define it and ascertain how much skill it requires. It is, he says, more like a *routine* than an *art*, and a routine that merely 'produces gratification and pleasure'.[4] Rhetoric produces only the appearance of knowledge, and cookery merely provides bodily pleasures, not the real pleasures of understanding. Socrates does not think very highly of rhetoric, or of cookery, for that matter. In this argument he is trying to distinguish rhetoric from philosophy – the appearance of truth from actual truth. Cookery and rhetoric are more like flattery, or a routine or a knack, he says.[5] Although *Gorgias* is not really about cooking per se, it is an analogy that is an easy reference to an activity that does not take much effort or understanding, and that emphasizes the *look* of a thing more than the thing itself.

Given that this is the most famous reference to cooking in the entire philosophical canon, it is clear why – if it is true that all philosophy is just a series of footnotes to Plato – it was never picked up as a serious subject of investigation.[6] Although we do not know a lot about cooking methods in Plato's day, we do know that he ate, and that Socrates, at least, loved to drink people under the table as a way of showing off his superior capacity for reason.[7] But we do know that food always played a part in political philosophy from the beginning, since working out where food would come from (via roads, railways and ports) was always an issue of the utmost importance in forming stable political entities. But this is not the same as cooking – the actual knowledge involved in preparing food.

The concepts Plato works with when he says that cooking does not require real knowledge are *episteme* (knowledge) and *techne* (art, craft, skill or knack). The domain of knowledge is theory, while the domain of craft is practice. Presumably, our own modern understandings of these concepts have coloured our view of them, but in general, theory and practice exist on two different sides of a divide that cannot be traversed. Theory is abstract and not concerned with particular problems or disciplines. Practice requires hands-on experience. Throughout his dialogues, Plato refers to several different disciplines as crafts: 'medicine, horsemanship, huntsmanship, oxherding, farming, calculation, geometry, generalship, piloting a ship, chariot-driving, political craft, prophecy, music, lyre-playing, flute-playing, painting, sculpture, housebuilding, shipbuilding, carpentry, weaving, pottery, smithing, and cookery'.[8] Each of these is associated with a practitioner – a doctor or musician, for example. But knowledge is something not necessarily demonstrated by *doing* so much as *understanding*. For Plato, knowledge can begin with doing, but not always. Socrates' teachings and most of Plato's writings are dedicated to the idea that through proper (Socratic) questioning and focused dialogue, that understanding is developed cognitively, not through practice. This is one of the distinctive features of Plato's epistemology. Understanding is something one has that can only be abstract, and rational. *Knowing that* something is true and *knowing how* to do something are two substantially different kinds of knowledge. For Plato at least, *episteme* (knowing that) is always the far superior form of knowledge. Using cooking as the primary metaphor for learning a craft (*techne*) might elucidate some of the ways in which Plato thought of this skill, but I do not think he thought of it as a skill with any real value. It might be of some *practical* value, but it is not about understanding or truth. This might be because food was not as interesting to the ancients as it is to us, but more likely because cooking was women's work. Plato never thought of cooking much at all, in all likelihood. All the skills he talks about in the above list were performed by men.

Since the initial division of the theoretical and the practical, philosophers regularly use this dichotomous hierarchy when approaching ways of knowing. That is, *understanding* is always thought to be superior to merely *doing*. We can do things by following instructions, or following rules, without knowing what we are doing or why we are doing it. I can follow a recipe without understanding how to cook, or how to season a dish, or why it needs to cook for a certain length of time. I can fill in a 'paint by numbers' painting without understanding the principles of design. At some point, however, knowing and doing can, and ideally should, become intertwined. One cannot have understanding without being able to demonstrate that understanding, and one only comes to full understanding from practice. Plato believed that theoretical understanding came from study, contemplation and dialogue, not from practice, but looking at the example of cooking can demonstrate that this is not the case.

The debate about theoretical and practical knowledge did not end with Plato. It is one of the central themes throughout philosophical history: we seem to be on a never-ending quest to accurately characterize how it is that we know different kinds of things. Cooking is an example that seems to fall clearly into the practical knowledge camp. One must be able to demonstrate that one knows how to cook by doing it, not by defining it or talking about it. These two categories, theoretical and practical, fail us in fully fleshing out the ways in which we think of cooking.

Knowledge and Cooking

Although many philosophers have spent a good part of their efforts trying to describe knowledge accurately, the twentieth-century philosopher Michael Oakeshott offers some useful descriptive categories that are more helpful than the typical theoretical/practical distinction. Oakeshott suggests that history, science, practice and the aesthetic are the four primary modes of knowing. Each of these is to be understood as distinct and conceptually different from the others, and each is important in different ways and for different reasons. According to him, 'a mode of experience implies a distinct and autonomous kind of understanding. It implies a universe of discourse with its own arguments and ways of assessing and grounding them.'[9] What this means is that each of these four ways of knowing has its own claims, different kinds of evidence and its own methods of proof. History reconstructs what has happened using a number of different kinds of source, building in narratives of cause, explanation and effects. But the accounts given afterwards can become invalid if the sources used are invalid, if the bias is too strong, or if there are parts intentionally left out to make the account appear drastically different than it should. Scientific understanding uses the scientific method for proof, where experiments are done and shown to be reproducible. Scientific claims must be falsifiable. Aesthetic experience is related to the ways in which we are moved by sensory experience. Art, literature and music all move us in different ways and have their own structures and criteria, but they cannot be judged in the way that history or science can.

Practice – hands-on creation – really should be considered its own form of knowledge, fundamentally different from the others. Practice is a 'bottom-up' approach that does not rely on theory, but rather encourages hands-on repetition in order to demonstrate skill. This might include the knowledge that an experienced carpenter has of how to build a table, or baker of when the bread has proved enough and is ready to go into the oven. There are skills that one cannot understand without this practice. Playing an instrument, for instance, requires repetition, feedback and hours of practice. There is no way to be a good player without knowing some music theory. However, lots of theory can never replace the hours of practice required to be a competent player.

Oakeshott's account is appealing. Most accounts of knowledge rely on strict and oversimplified dichotomies characterized either by the theoretical and the practical,[10] the *a priori* and *a posteriori* (prior to experience or after experience),[11] or explicit and tacit knowledge (things that are easy to articulate and things gained from experience that might be harder to express). These dichotomies force us into thinking not only about knowledge as an either/or, but that two 'kinds' of knowledge might not have anything to do with each other. The ways we make sense of how things work, and how and why things might be true, are necessarily interrelated. Theoretically we can separate them out into neat categories, but in reality it is impossible to do so. If I memorize all of the rules to basketball, and take a course in physics in order to understand the trajectory of basketballs, there is no reason to think I can get an actual basketball into a net. Conversely, if I play basketball for hours every day but I don't understand the rules, it is not likely that I will be any good, since I don't know what counts and what doesn't count. I need both the understanding *and* the practice. 'Hands-on' professions such as plumbing certainly require practice and experience, but they also require deep understanding. In the case of plumbing it is necessary to understand water, gravity, pressure, different materials (copper vs plastic, for example) and the way any number of large plumbing systems work.

Oakeshott rejects accounts that allow for what he calls rationalism, or a form of knowledge that allows for axioms or principles that are said to come from reason alone. He contends that nothing can be known without experience, as this is the nature of the human mind. He explains that we understand by interacting with the world around us, and any 'knowledge that is identified as rational is itself really a product of experience and judgement. It consists of rules, methods, or techniques abstracted from practice – tools that, far from being substitutes for experience and judgement, cannot be effectively used in their absence.'[12] Thus he stands with a number of other philosophers who reject *a priori* knowledge (literally 'before experience', something that can be known innately), including Aristotle, John Locke, David Hume and George Berkeley. What makes Oakeshott different from these others is the real recognition that there are multiple kinds of knowing beyond the practical and theoretical.

Cooking requires *both* theoretical and practical knowledge. Because it is important to get a 'feel' for a large number of variables in a kitchen, it can take years to learn. As one chef said, 'It's not the clock that tells you when it's done; the food does.'[13] Experienced bakers know when their bread is done because it smells a certain way. Experienced cooks know that oven temperatures vary, altitude changes things in the oven, and flour varies tremendously depending on how finely it is milled or how old it is. Experienced cooks taste at several stages of cooking to ensure that the flavour is right, and adjust accordingly. They do not rely entirely on a recipe to know that a dish will come out exactly as planned. Good cooks taste, smell and feel food constantly. They know when flour has gone stale by touching it, when spices have gone dull or flat by smelling them, and when a little extra seasoning is needed to brighten up a dish by tasting it. They know when a squeeze of lemon juice can help, and why lime juice might ruin the same dish. Good cooks know what bread dough feels like in their hands as it develops into a loaf that is ready to bake. They can look in a pantry or a refrigerator and understand how to put together a meal with a variety of things that may not look like much to anyone else. The knowledge to be able to do all of these things requires a combination of experiences with the senses as well as practice at actually making food.

Recipes as Rulebooks

The words 'recipe' and 'receipt' both come from the same Latin root word *recipere*, which can mean either 'to take' or 'to receive'. In her 1922 book on etiquette, Emily Post wrote that in reference to social usage, '*receipt* has a more distinguished ancestry, but since *recipe* is used by all modern writers on cooking, only [difficult people] insist on *receipt*.'[14] Recipes were a form of written evidence of what it was that you had eaten. Recipes and receipts are connected by the way they point to, or *refer* to, the things received. But recipes are really a relatively new development, historically speaking, only becoming common in the early twentieth century. Before written recipes, young women would learn to cook alongside their mothers, learning how to make various dishes and how to approximate the amounts of different ingredients. If you did not learn to cook at home, it was difficult to learn on your own just through experimentation.

American author Rick Bragg recently published a book with stories and recipes from his mother's kitchen.[15] Rick's mother Margaret's approach to cooking was informed by her own mother and her grandfather before her (her grandfather loved sweet biscuits and perfected his own recipe). Margaret grew up in the rural south and cooked with traditional ingredients, and anything that was available (she didn't like to cook with squirrel brains as they were too metallic-tasting, she said). Like many women for hundreds of years, Margaret did not use a cookbook. She did not even own one. She did not use recipes. She used a fork and a spoon (which, her son jokes, were likely forged during the Mexican-American war). No mixer, no blender. She had a favourite cast-iron pan that she had seasoned to perfection. After a house fire, a relative offered to buy her a new one. She refused, saying it would take her the rest of her life to get a new one seasoned properly, and she went through the rubble of the fire to get her old pan back. Margaret said, 'A person can't cook from a book ... a person can't cook from numbers.'[16] She explained, 'You learn by tasting and feeling and smelling and listening and remembering, and burning things now and then, and singing the right songs.'[17] Margaret did not own measuring cups or measuring spoons. As Bragg describes, his mother's cooking lexicon included 'part of a handful', 'a handful' and 'a real good handful'.[18] Margaret Bragg learned to cook by *feel*, not by rules or books. Not everyone needs to cook like this, but this is the way that women were taught to cook for thousands of years.

In America Fannie Farmer changed all of that for women across the country. Farmer was born in the mid-nineteenth century and went to the Boston Cooking School when she was thirty. She excelled at the school and in a short time became its director. What Farmer did in that role was to standardize the measurements of food, which had never been done before, and then developed strict written instructions for individual recipes. According to Farmer: 'Correct measurements are absolutely necessary to insure the best results. Good judgement, with experience, has taught some to measure by sight; but the majority need definite guidelines.'[19] And she reiterates repeatedly: '*A cupful is measured level. A tablespoonful is measured level. A teaspoonful is measured level.*'[20] Of course she also invented, or at least standardized, the measurements themselves. Before Farmer, measurements in recipes approximated sizes that cooks would have an easy reference to, for example, 'a piece of butter the size of an egg', or 'a finger length of cheese'. Lots of comparisons would be to the human hand, or of things that would be common in many kitchens, such as a walnut or a saucer. 'A teacup of flour' became a cup. And one cup became the same across the country, emanating from Farmer's Boston Cooking School and her cookbooks. Teaspoons, tablespoons and cups became standardized for Americans, along with quarts, pints and gallons. Farmer became 'the mother of level measurements'. Her entire approach 'was about offering cooks a sense that they could do anything, so long as they obeyed the rules and followed her instructions to the letter: absolute obedience would lead to absolute proficiency'.[21] Measurements and recipes allowed for a cook to make the same dish repeatedly without wondering if would be the same every time. (The rest of the world seems to have standardized measures by weight, which is actually a much more precise way to measure than the American model.)

But there were many more elements to cooking that needed to become standardized before recipes could really make their way into every kitchen: oven temperatures, mixing techniques, cooking times (and it was not until the 1950s that most American kitchens had wall clocks) and the standardization of ingredients, to begin with. As fewer women learned to cook beside their own mothers because of war, the Great Depression or because their mothers went out to work, women relied more on recipes than they had in the nineteenth century. Cookbooks became more widely available and more women were literate. Since the advent of refrigeration in homes, refrigerated trucks and supermarkets, more food could be kept in the home without going bad. With the advent of processed food, packaged food can be kept (almost) indefinitely and requires little to no skill to prepare and heat (particularly if you have a microwave).

But when a cook has to rely on recipes, they end up dependent on a kind of strict instruction that knowing how to cook does not require. Julia Child echoed this sentiment in an interview later in her life when she said, 'You learn to cook so that you don't have to be a slave to recipes. You get what's in season and you know what to do with it.'[22] With the rise of restaurants, processed food and fast (and cheap) food, women could cook less and less, but along with that ease came a cultural deskilling – an actual loss of the cultural knowledge that cooking requires. In the twenty-first century many people (not just women) do not have the vaguest idea of how to cook food from scratch, what they might do with unprocessed ingredients like whole chickens, red peppers or even carrots. (In a cooking class I taught once, I had a college student remark that she had never seen a 'full-size' carrot; she only knew about the 'baby-size'.)

Recipes also have a legal status. Although they can only have what is called a 'thin copyright', it is the narrative instructions, not the list of ingredients, that carries some legal status. The list of ingredients can be put together so many ways that they cannot constitute any sort of unified entity that could be proprietary. Neither can *tastes* be copyrighted, as was determined by the Court of Justice of the European Union. In a case over the taste of two herbed cream cheeses, 'witches' cheese' from one brand and 'wise women's cheese' from another, it was determined that the taste of a food product cannot be copyrighted. These two cheeses tasted very similar, even though their ingredients were different. In 2007 in the Netherlands, a court decided that the list of *ingredients* did not matter as much as the overall taste of a cheese, but that 'the *taste* of a food product *cannot* be classified as a "work".'[23] A 'work' is like an artwork: in order to be able to understand it, make laws about it or put a price on it, we need to understand what constitutes it.

In aesthetics, there is a general division between what we call the static arts and the performance of performing arts. Static arts, like painting or sculpture, focus on a physical object that does not move or change. Performing arts, such as dance, music or theatre, generally have a score or a script whereby the performance is some sort of instantiation of that set of instructions. The 'work' in the performing arts is more slippery, given that a script does not seem to be the work, nor does a singular performance. It seems likely that it is actually a misnomer to want to say that there is a 'work' in the same way that there is in the static arts. But the work is still what we attach legal status to. So it is not the list of ingredients, *nor* is it the taste of a food, but the narrative description or instructions which outline the steps to making a dish that is eligible for ownership or copyright status.

Imagine a recipe for chocolate chip cookies. The cookies come out very differently if the butter is melted or hard, or if you cream the butter and sugar before the rest of the ingredients are added. The list of ingredients is the same, but the narrative instruction might tell you to do things in very different ways, and this influences the way the dish comes out. Mayonnaise is another example where the ingredients hardly dictate results if you do not follow the instructions properly. The oil has to be added very slowly to the egg as it is being whisked, otherwise it will not emulsify properly and the result is not mayonnaise but an eggy, oily mess (I know this one from personal experience).

Generally, copyrights protect works or expressions, but not ideas. The U.S. determined that 'a mere listing of ingredients is not protected under copyright law. However, where a recipe or formula is accompanied by substantial literary expression in the form of an explanation or directions, or when there is a collection of recipes as in a cookbook, there may be a basis for copyright protection.'[24] Whereas recipes have never really needed to be understood as commodities before, in this new age of litigation and celebrity chefs they have become just that. Anne Thornton, an 'expert pastry chef' and the host of a Food Network show called *Dessert First*, which launched in October 2010, was accused of plagiarizing a few recipes from the likes of Ina Garten and Martha Stewart. Specifically, what got her into trouble were her lemon squares, which too closely resembled Garten's lemon squares from her *Barefoot Contessa* cookbook. When asked about the originality of her recipes, Thornton said that when it comes to 'lemon squares, there's only so many ways you can make them, so of course there will be similarities.'[25] Thornton's show was cancelled, but she claims it was because of low ratings, not because of the plagiarized recipes. In Canada, Caroline Dumas accused chef Danny St Pierre of recipe plagiarism during a live interview radio show. Dumas had created a *pudding-chômeur*, a traditional cake from Quebec (a cross between bread pudding and sticky toffee), a recipe for which St Pierre posted on the website for his restaurant *Auguste*. St Pierre was seriously taken aback to be charged with this live on the air, but he claimed ignorance that recipe plagiarism was a problem and has since given attribution to Dumas on his website with this disclaimer: 'Warning: pudding-chômeur is a heritage recipe. This modern adaptation is in line with one initiated by Caroline Dumas.'[26] In general, giving attribution is always a safer option than pretending the recipe came out of nowhere if you publish it or sell it.

This 'thin copyright' status is pretty dubious when it comes to recipes specifically. Given that recipes have never really required strict attribution, it is historically anomalous that we can now file lawsuits and people can lose jobs over plagiarizing recipes. There seem to be two camps on this issue: those who believe that recipes can never be owned and that attribution should never be needed, and those who believe that recipes should be treated like intellectual property and can be infringed on and plagiarized.[27] There is a lot of history on intellectual property infringement for things other than recipes, but it looks as if recipes will end up taking the same legal status as poetry, where the words themselves are considered to be the intellectual property, and not the meaning, intention or effect. The words are the written form of the 'work' in question. What strikes me as so odd about this is that with recipes the work ends up being the written instructions, not the list of ingredients, the food itself or the taste. Presumably both of the latter would be too difficult to pin down in the ways that copyright laws are written, and so the essence of a recipe becomes the narrative description of how it is made, not its contents, flavour or nutritional value.

Breaking the Rules

In the preface to her cookbook *How to Eat*, Nigella Lawson begins by saying: 'Cooking is not just about joining the dots, following one recipe slavishly and then moving on to the next. It's about developing an understanding of food, [and] a sense of assurance in the kitchen.'[28] Following rules with no understanding does not produce good food, and it does not produce a happy cook. Presumably, many people cook merely by slavishly following recipes without ever coming to understand the underlying principles of why certain foods behave in the ways that they do or why some things taste good together and others do not. But those who learn from a teacher (or a mother) learn to get a 'feel' for what textures, flavours and aromas *should* come from cooking certain things. This is something that can only come from experience; from doing, and not just theoretical understanding. According to Lawson, learning to cook is as much about finding what food pleases you as it is about conquering the form of transformation that the skill entails. 'The easiest way to cook,' she writes, 'is by watching.'[29] For her, cooking should start at one's own stove; you learn from both *watching* and then from *doing*:

> Chefs themselves know this. The great chefs from France and Italy learn about food at home; what they do later, in the restaurants that make them famous, is use what they have learned. They build on it, they start elaborating. They take home cooking to the restaurant, not the restaurant school of cooking to the home. Inverting the process is like learning the vocabulary without any grammar.[30]

Grammar is the 'glue' that gives words meaning. Vocabulary without meaning is like having a garage full of tools that you do not know how to use. And there is no point in having a refrigerator full of food that you cannot make into a meal if you do not eventually come to an understanding of how it works.

In philosophical ethics, there are a number of ways to determine what the 'right' thing to do is in any given circumstance. There is a whole category of 'rule-based' ethics, which begin with a rule, which just needs to be applied to different kinds of circumstances. Kantian ethics have the 'categorical imperative', which contends that you should only act in ways that you could make your action a universal law: if it would be OK for everyone to do it, then it is OK for you to do it. This is the reverse of the golden rule, which says that if you do it, then it would be OK for everyone to do it. John Stuart Mill gave a different rule, which said that good actions should maximize good outcomes and minimize harms, and that everyone should be counted equally. He calls this the principle of utility: it is the foundation of utilitarianism. The Ten Commandments are also an early form of rule-based ethics. Follow the rules in order to be a good person, and then you will be allowed to live within a community. Rule-based ethics came about largely in the Enlightenment, when thinkers were trying to come up with a system of morality that did not depend on religious belief. It seemed, to them, that there could be a universal system of morality that was based in reason and would work for people of all faiths.

Before rule-based ethics existed there were virtue ethics, started by Aristotle. He argued that everything we did as humans was directed at some goal or some good. Behaving well is directed towards being virtuous and ultimately towards living the most fulfilled life possible. But people do not know how to behave well

by nature, he says, and we have to be taught. And we are taught
to behave, according to Aristotle, at our mother's knee. Cooking
works the same way. Many people learn to cook by their mother's
(or father's) side (though many now do not, because home cooking is becoming more and more rare). But cooking is like virtue
ethics, in that it is goal-orientated (serving up good meals) but
the path to get there can come in any number of forms. For
Aristotle, there are a number of different skills that one must
develop when one is learning to become good. First of all, good
actions are never done accidentally. You have to know what it is
that you are doing, why you are doing it and that you are doing
it at the right time. For all those things to happen, you have to
be aware of the situation and you have to understand the ramifi-
cations of your actions. Aristotle says that acting virtuously must
become a habit, because it is not inborn. Children are taught to
say please and thank you and it becomes habit. As they grow into
adults they do not have to think about what the polite thing to
say is when they are handed something. An Aristotelian version
of virtue cooking begins with watching someone else do it, practising doing it yourself, getting the *feel* of what a cup of flour feels
like. You get a *feel* of what biscuit dough feels like, and you get
a *feel* of what colours, smells and textures are supposed to be
when food is cooked successfully. When you know what the right
amount feels like, then you begin to know how to use certain
ingredients repeatedly and reliably. I make bread every week. I
have a recipe that I use, but as I have done this so many times now,
I do not need to look at the recipe any more. I know what the
bread should feel like and look like at each stage of the process.
When my kids help with the bread, I use the recipe so that they
can start with strict measurements, so that they too will eventually get to know what each ingredient looks and feels like, and

when the dough might need a bit more flour or, God forbid, we have added too much salt.

What happens when you do not learn to trust yourself with cooking is that you continue to be a rule-based cook, not knowing when substitutions might be allowed, how to adjust for five diners rather than four, or what happens when all your spices have gone flat (I have seen many a cupboard with a twenty-year-old tin of nutmeg). Cooking is never merely a mathematical equation or a scientific formula. It is, rather, a *process*. And, as with virtue ethics, knowing how to cook involves the *understanding* of the ways in which foods combine and the ways in which food transforms through practice. In the same sense that virtue ethics is always reaching towards a certain ideal, the more practice one gets, the better one is at doing it. The same goes for cooking. There is no ideal sauce, and there are always more meals to cook (although the French might argue that there are five ideal mother sauces, and knowing those is the foundation of good French cooking). But developing the knowledge required for habitually cooking good food requires the same kind of study, watching, experience and feedback that becoming virtuous does, according to Aristotle.

Part of the reason why cooking cannot be strictly rule-based is because we cook according to what tastes good to us. Individual tastes vary, and of course so do cultural tastes. Furthermore, the variables that one uses in the kitchen are never completely stable. But cooking should not be about strict rules. It is, rather, about principles. In her book *How to Eat*, originally published in 1998, Lawson essentially encouraged women in particular to think about home cooking with more pleasure. This meant that they needed to cook what was good to them, what they liked and what was fun to make, rather than seeing it as drudgery. This book, and Lawson's attitude, was a direct throwback to 1970s second-wave feminism, which rejected the notion that women should find their primary identity and happiness in being a homemaker. Lawson saw that cooking had become dreaded work for many women, and she thought they deserved to find some joy in it. Her follow-up book *How to Be a Domestic Goddess*, an ironic title, again offered an invitation to women to *bake* things they liked without feeling under pressure to make perfect confections in a home kitchen:

> The trouble with much modern cooking is not that the food it produces isn't good, but that the mood it induces in the cook is one of skin-of-the-teeth efficiency, all briskness and little pleasure. Sometimes that's the best we can manage, but at other times we don't want to feel like a postmodern, postfeminist, overstretched woman but, rather, like a domestic goddess, trailing nutmeggy fumes of baking pie in our languorous wake.[31]

The point is not to *be* a domestic goddess, but to *feel* like one.

Lawson was releasing her cookbooks not long after her American counterpart, Martha Stewart, who really did want to give American women a platform to become domestic goddesses, began to write in the 1980s. This was about the time of the full downfall of home cooking, and a rejection of proper etiquette came to a head. Stewart published her first cookbook, *Entertaining*, in 1982, destined to become one of the best-selling cookbooks of all time. But Stewart's dishes were complex and time-consuming, and she offered advice on how to cook brunch for more guests than most people can seat in their house ('a midnight omelet supper for thirty' or 'an Italian buffet for fifty'). Her cooking show, which premiered in 1993, became wildly successful as a way to teach housewives how to domesticate properly. But Stewart is a much stricter cook than Lawson, or the sometimes bumbling Julia Child, who seemed to be learning to cook alongside her viewers – at least early on. In *Entertaining*, Stewart even describes how to make scrambled eggs: 'Ever since I was small I have loved scrambled eggs, but generally *only* as my mother made them – fresh eggs, lightly beaten with a fork and cooked in melted sweet butter – nothing added.'[32] The recipe she gives, though, is for forty guests and uses eighty eggs.

Ultimately, of course, people are free to cook the way they choose – with no recipes or kitchen gadgets like Margaret Bragg, with strict measuring tools like Fannie Farmer, or with a real sense of joy and fun like Nigella Lawson. There is no one way to cook, just as there is no one way to be moral. But there are cooking failures, just as there are moral failures, when one cannot master basic principles, when one has no thought or care for others or when one has such disregard for the whole endeavour that one rejects engaging with cooking altogether, relying on microwave meals, restaurants and takeaways. But just as there are many ways to cook, and many ways to learn, one cannot reject out of hand the importance of the transformation of food and the role it plays in all our lives.

Cookbooks as Ideologies

Usually we think of ideologies as connected to political systems, educational systems or religions. The way we choose to eat often involves these invisible or unspoken beliefs as well. Vegetarians follow a rule not to eat meat. The reason behind that rule may be for animal welfare, environmental reasons, health reasons, religious or cultural reasons, or just plain palatability. But in order to subscribe to the ideology of vegetarianism, one must have a particular set of beliefs. Someone who claims to be a vegetarian should be able to talk about the reasons and beliefs that they have for choosing not to eat meat. Cookbooks are often part of an ideological system in the way that they advocate a particular way of thinking about the foods they describe. Authors carefully select specific recipes to form a coherent account of some particular way of cooking, and in turn, a way of thinking about food. Some cookbooks are made to teach the fundamentals of cooking, some to advocate a particular diet, and some to teach a particular cultural cuisine. Given that cookbooks can shed a lot of light on what is happening in a culture, they are one of the sources that historians often use to collect information about the cooking tendencies of a nation.

Irma Rombauer's *Joy of Cooking* is the most popular American cookbook in history (with over 20 million copies sold since 1931). It features simple recipes that middle-class Americans should be able to cook, along with Rombauer's directions and witty commentary. The *Joy of Cooking* helped several generations of home cooks master the basics of typical American fare. The ideology that it promotes includes basic cooking techniques, clear explanations of how ingredients interact with one another, and the most important underlying argument: that cooking should be fun and engaging, and as joyful as the meal itself. In the foreword, Rombauer writes that by using her comprehensive cookbook, the home cook should be able to experience 'unexpected triumphs', 'actually revel in a new-found freedom', and 'regain the priceless private joy of family living, dining, and sharing.'[33] Maybe this is a lot to expect from a cookbook, but this book really is comprehensive in its scope: it shows the home cook how to do everything from setting the table properly to mapping out different cuts of meat. It is a how-to manual on calories, food additives, why cooking from scratch is nutritionally better and preserving foods long-term so they retain their nutrition, and it includes hundreds of sample menus that are nutritionally rounded out for family or entertaining. Surely it was an important manual for women as they were tasked with cooking for families, and for learning to entertain.

Joy, as it is referred to in the shorthand, came out at the beginning of the Great Depression but its nine subsequent revisions have tried to keep up with all of the phases of economic development as well as all three waves of feminism and the changing attitudes towards the role of women in the kitchen. It dropped a whole chapter on wartime rationing and added one on frozen desserts.[34] The book is a ubiquitous graduation or wedding present, and it is common in many American homes. Just as many of our most firmly held beliefs sometimes become invisible to us, this book and the lessons it teaches have been the backbone of American cuisine for almost a hundred years. Another underlying assumption about its ideology is that there should, or even could, be a single book so comprehensive (with over 4,300 recipes) that all of American cooking, entertaining and preserving is summed up in it.

To understand the importance of cooking, we cannot turn to the history of philosophy, but we can borrow philosophical concepts to make sense of what it is people do to transform their groceries into dinner. One of the ways we might begin to investigate is to look at the history of cookbooks, which can give us insight into the ways cooks have left a legacy of written instructions, at least, of their recipes and techniques. According to Henry Notaker, author of *A History of Cookbooks*, people were writing down cooking instructions as early as 3,500 years ago.[35]

That far back, recipes had to be carved into stone, of course. They were lists of ingredients, unfortunately with no detailed instructions. These recipes were mostly for meat stews that were to be made as offerings to the gods in the temples.

The first printed cookbook came out in Rome in around 1470: *On Honest Indulgence and Good Health* (*De honesta voluptate et valetudine*) by Bartolomeo Sacchi, also known as Bartolomeo Platina after his birthplace (Piadena) in Italy. Platina borrowed recipes from his friend Master Martino da Como, and although this book included more than 250 dishes, Platina was as much focused on presenting a way of thinking of food as on instructions for its preparation. He included a 'systematic discussion of the art of cooking, nutrition (related to the usefulness of regular physical activity), food hygiene, the ethics of eating, and the pleasures of the table, according to practical and moral prescriptions about food and eating.[36] Platina was a devoted 'humanist' who advocated unapologetically that eating, and the pleasure we derive from it, was 'among the legitimate components of a person's existential balance.[37] He advocated moderation, of course, which he said would lead to happiness. He said that food should never be considered sinful, but that you should not overdo it. The relationship between food and pleasure, and food and gluttony, has long been a topic of concern for religions and governments and it is rare not to see some indications that moderation is often a goal.

Looking at cookbooks as sources of historical information about what people were eating a few hundred years ago can be an interesting exercise, but given that such books are few and far between, they give a skewed view of past recipes. Many cookbooks highlight what would have been available in the local landscape, teaching us what kinds of meat were consumed, how readily available cheese or dairy might have been, and what the use was of ingredients we might have thought common but were, in fact, not all that common. Tomatoes, for example, are thought to be ubiquitous in Italian cuisine, but they were not imported from the u.s. to Italy until the sixteenth century. Tomato *sauce* was not developed until the mid-eighteenth century, by chef Francesco Leonardi.[38] Early on, other exotic ingredients would have only been available to royalty or the extremely wealthy. Many cookbooks were written for them, and it was their recipes that were collected, so they do not always give us a good sense of what *most* people ate in a given time. Given that a total of only 174 cookbooks were published before 1700, it appears that the written recipe only came about long after the advent of all kinds of local and regional cuisines.

Since the beginning, cookbooks were not just collections of recipes, but were often ideological treatises that advocate a particular way of eating and living. They include some foods and purposefully leave others out. They advocate certain health benefits or the look of certain dishes as indicative of resource-fulness, or being loving, or extravagant – whichever one you are going for. Ancient Greek philosopher Pythagoras was a known cult leader who advocated a vegetarian diet but warned of the dangers of eating beans (he thought them to be closely con-nected to the souls of the dead and that eating them was a form of cannibalism). Sylvester Graham (of graham cracker fame) also advocated vegetarianism, but with healthy doses of wholegrain wheat. Graham's friend Harvey Kellogg (of Kellogg cereals and the director of the Battle Creek Sanitarium) advocated strict veg-etarianism, strict sexual abstinence (masturbation was thought to be especially harmful), a regime of daily yoghurt enemas and, of course, wholegrain corn flakes, which were developed as part of his healthy diet. Today we can find cookbooks for all kinds of diets and lifestyles, from the Mediterranean diet (which was actually recognized by the UNESCO Intangible Heritage List in 2010,[39] rich in extra virgin olive oil, fish, vegetables and whole grains), to Paleo diets (AKA the caveman diet, heavy on unprocessed meat and root vegetables but no post-industrial products), to so-called 'clean eating' (which emphasizes no processed foods, alcohol, caffeine or sugar, with the added implication that foods not included in the diet are *unclean*). Each of these diets insists that it is not a *diet* but a *lifestyle*, and that it will have an incredible impact on one's state of mind (usually clearer thinking and increased ability to focus) and one's overall state of physical health (always more energy). The cookbooks often come with specialized tools or measuring devices.

Cookbooks are often indicative of food trends. They are great roadmaps of what people would typically have in their households, but given that this is so temporal and so regional, the cookbooks tend to be too. In one cookbook from 1922 called *Things Mother Used to Make*, ingredients include many things not typically found in a modern (American) kitchen, such as sour milk, graham flour, yeast cake (or cake yeast, a form of liquid yeast good only for making cakes) and Indian meal.[40] In the American South, many cookbooks came about from ingredients and methods that African slaves brought to the U.S., such as rice cultivation, red peas and okra.[41] These foods became emblematic of what we now call soul food and a lot of Southern food. The cover of one cookbook from the early 1900s, *Southern Recipes*, boasts a cartoon drawing of a Black mammy ringing a dinner bell with two Black children running to her.[42] Although this would be considered offensive now, it is probably reflective of the fact that Black women were doing the bulk of the cooking for Southern white families, and many of their recipes were likely woven into the history of the traditional recipes of the American South. The recipes in this book, however, are handwritten by women who were all members of the Montgomery, Alabama Junior League, and presumably they were all white. Over three hundred pages of recipes have been put together in this book to show how to embody Southern hospitality, from cocktails and canapés to poultry and preserves. The recipes are meals that Black women would have cooked so the white hospitality could happen.

Contemporary Southern cookbook author Paula Deen is well known for her love of butter in cooking. She was the Southern emblem for the rejection of low-fat cooking, claiming that it diminished the flavour of Southern food. But after being diagnosed with diabetes, her son Bobby Deen reined in the cooking fats and put forward a much more health-conscious balance of recipes. 'Bobby's Remakes', or 'Bobby's Lighter Recipes', revise his mother's recipes and suggest substitutions for the high-calorie and high-fat ingredients, claiming that his versions add flavour and eliminate many of the calories.[43]

Given that we just do have ideological beliefs about what we eat, whether it be vegetarianism, carnism or even flexitarianism, the ideas and ideals we commit to have a lot to do with the ways in which we interact with the world around us (and perhaps whether or not we eat animals). These beliefs are influenced by our culture, family, education, exposure to different foods and so on. But the ideologies that rule the decisions that we make about eating, even though they are largely unarticulated by many people, are the set of beliefs that determine what we choose to put in our mouths.

Cooking as Epistemology

Imagine that cooking is the foundation of an epistemology, or a way of knowing, or even the model for a basis of inquiry. Some cookbooks help us to think about meals that can be made quickly; some help us make meals that avoid gluten or carbohydrates. Each cookbook helps us to think about cooking from a particular viewpoint, just as each philosopher makes arguments about how to 'see' and approach the world in a particular way. But cookbooks are not mere sets of instructions or lists of recipes: they are born out of the experience of a cook. A cookbook is the instruction that is meant to stand in for a teacher or a mother. Most are accompanied by commentary, reflections on what has worked in the past for the cook and what has not, and reasons why they have included a particular recipe in their book.

Lisa Heldke addressed just this kind of thing when she asked, 'Could it ever make sense to think of cooking as a form of inquiry?'[44] She suggests that many people tend to think only in terms of objectivism and relativism. Objectivism takes the approach that there is a static world outside us to understand, and we can have certain knowledge of that world. Relativism is the view that knowledge must be understood in terms of context, relations, culture or theoretical framework. She refers to the dichotomy between these two as 'Cartesian indecision', or 'the conviction that either there is a firm foundation for our knowledge, *or* we are condemned to swirl endlessly in the morass of intellectual and moral indecision.'[45] Usually these are categories we use when thinking about ethics, and whether morality is absolute or context dependent, but the debate is important in the ways we think about other kinds of knowledge as well. Heldke suggests, however, that neither option is all that accurate in practical thinking about how people actually live and know. She puts forward a third way of approaching knowledge, calling it the 'Co-responsible Option'.[46] She rejects the hierarchical approach where the 'knower' approaches some sort of external, unknown problem. Instead, she suggests that we 'think of inquiry as a communal activity, [and] that we emphasize the relationships that obtain between inquirers and inquired'.[47] This is, of course, born out of a feminist approach to knowledge acquisition which rejects hierarchical knowledge as a form of domination. Heldke notes that the language of epistemology is couched almost entirely in scientific terms, which tends to be dominated by men. But cooking, and its terms, methods and physical space, is one that is almost entirely dominated by women. So what happens if we use *cooking* as a method of inquiry, instead of science? We find an approach that is much more inclusive of multiple participants and differing experiences, and the idea that there are better and worse ways to do things in the kitchen. There are multiple ways to attain similar results with different tools and methods.

John Dewey, the early twentieth-century American pragmatist, said that inquiry was 'the controlled or directed transformation of an indeterminate situation into one that is so determinate in its constituent distinctions and relations as to convert the elements of the original situation into a unified whole'.[48] In other words, an inquiry should ascertain how something uncertain can transform into something certain or determinate, and how all the fragments become integrated into a unified whole. This need not be reduced into merely the chemistry of food or chemical change; rather, we can look at cooking as a primary and familiar way in which we think about wonder, experimentation, reproducibility and success. Cooking provides a basis for understanding measurement, weight, volume, heat and saturation. But we do not cook to learn scientific or chemical principles, but to make dinner and to feed our families and ourselves. We cook to demonstrate love, and the best kitchens have an attitude of collaboration.

Cooking as inquiry allows for a different kind of approach to understanding what it means to *know* and what it means to master a domain of knowledge. If the goal of inquiry is understanding, as Dewey says, to move from the uncertain to the certain, cooking demonstrates this repeatedly. For everyone I have talked about in this chapter, from Margaret Bragg, who never used a 'rulebook' or a measuring device, to Fannie Farmer, who felt the need to standardize measuring devices for a country, cooking is something that one has to learn for oneself. Some people never learn to cook, just as some people never learn the basics of biology. But one can get by in this world without understanding biology; no one can get by without eating. Eating and cooking are obviously not the same, but they are fundamentally linked. We learn to cook from others, we cook with others, and we often teach others to cook in turn. Heldke suggests that theories and recipes are alike because they are both used to do things. She notes:

> The range of things that we may do with them is at least
> as broad as the range of things one may do with recipes.
> I may develop a theory to help myself tolerate a situation
> in which I find myself, or to explain to myself and others
> a set of experiences I've had. I may take up and modify
> a theory in order to help me develop a relationship with
> another person or persons. I may create a theory in order
> to have something to write about in a paper for a class.[49]

Theories are explanations, and the explanations that we use to make sense of our experiences are largely influenced by our own ideologies. My ability to create a meal out of a set of ingredients is dependent not only on the kinds of experiences I have had in the past, but on the ways in which I have had successes and failures with certain foods.

Recognizing cooking as a form of inquiry is in line with the tradition of feminist epistemology, which examines the ways in which women think and know differently from men, and ethno-epistemology, which examines the ways of knowing of various cultures. Cooking epistemology gives both experienced home cooks and accomplished chefs a place of honour as the experts of the kitchen. The body of knowledge that skilled chefs have is not in mathematical axioms or scientific reproducibility; rather, 'the proof of the pudding is in the eating,' as the old proverb goes. Theories and formulas become useless if one cannot execute a dish properly, and the knowledge and methods used to do that well constitute their own form of knowledge.

WENDELL BERRY famously claimed that 'eating is an agricultural act.'[50] What he meant by this is that eating food is an intentional act that connects us to the land in ways that we may or may not think about or even be aware of. But eating is a domestic act as well, since the food one eats is usually prepared by someone, even when that person may be invisible to us. Many of our meals are cooked in the home and the cook is someone we know and love, but a lot of meals are made in factories by people we cannot see and are not intended to even think about. Food made in factories is a very recent phenomenon: for most of human history, food had to be made by someone with the skill to cook the raw ingredients into something palatable. The skill that it takes to produce a decent meal for a family or a crowd is significant and the people who can do this well should be given due credit. Eating is only the last part of a long process that begins in the fields and is continued by people with the knowledge of how to transform raw ingredients. This ability to transform – the knowledge, one might say – is not incidental, it is not inherent and it is not insignificant. Cooking – and our tasting and enjoyment of cooked food, a meal – embodies one of the most substantial changes in raw material that happens in our lives. The knowledge that it takes to do that well is as substantial as any other form of knowledge.

References

Introduction

1 Jean Anthelme Brillat-Savarin, *The Physiology of Taste; or, Meditations on Transcendental Gastronomy*, trans. M.F.K. Fisher (New York, 1949), p. 15.
2 Adam Gopnik, *The Table Comes First: Family, France, and the Meaning of Food* (New York, 2012), p. 114.
3 Melvin Cherno, 'Feuerbach's "Man is what He Eats": A Rectification', *Journal of the History of Ideas*, XXIV/3 (1963), p. 401. A direct translation is 'man is what he eats'; I have changed it to make it more inclusive.
4 Alan Levinovitz, *The Gluten Lie: And Other Myths about What You Eat* (New York, 2015), p. 72.
5 Michael Pollan, *In Defense of Food: An Eater's Manifesto* (New York, 2008).
6 Constance Classen, 'The Senses', in *Encyclopedia of European Social History*, vol. IV: *Gender/Family and Ages/Sexuality/Body and Mind/Work* (Detroit, MI, 2001), pp. 355–64.

1 Good Taste and Bad Taste

1 'Taste, n.1', OED Online, www-oed-com, accessed 6 March 2020.
2 Roger Scruton, 'Architectural Taste', *British Journal of Aesthetics*, XV (Autumn 1975), p. 294.
3 *Huffington Post*, 'Cilantro Aversion Linked to Gene for Smell, New Study Finds', www.huffpost.com, 20 September 2012.
4 Alexander Baumgarten, *Metaphysics*, trans. Courtney D. Fugate and John Hymers (London, 2013), section 451.
5 David Hume, 'Of The Standard of Taste', in *Essays Moral, Political, and Literary* (Indianapolis, IN, 1987), section 8.
6 Ibid., section 15.

7 Alex Aronson, 'The Anatomy of Taste', *Modern Language Notes*, LXI/4 (April 1946), p. 229.

8 Ibid.

9 *Common Sense*, 'Of Taste in its proper Sense, and the Abuse of it among the Quality' (11 February 1738), quoted in Aronson, 'The Anatomy of Taste', p. 232, my italics.

10 Robert Solomon, 'On Kitsch and Sentimentality', *Journal of Aesthetics and Art Criticism*, XLIX/1 (Winter 1991), pp. 1–14.

11 Immanuel Kant, *Groundwork of the Metaphysics of Morals*, trans. H. J. Patton (New York, 1964), p. 13.

12 Pierre Bourdieu, 'From *Distinction*', in *Aesthetics: The Big Questions*, ed. Carolyn Korsmeyer (Malden, MA, 1998), p. 150.

13 Massimo Montanari, *Cheese, Pears and History in a Proverb*, trans. Beth Archer Brombert (New York, 2010), pp. 63–6.

14 Ibid., p. 65.

15 Julian Baggini, *The Virtues of the Table: How to Eat and Think* (London, 2014), p. 215.

16 Museum of Bad Art, http://museumofbadart.org, accessed 1 February 2021; Solomon, 'On Kitsch and Sentimentality', p. 1.

17 Ibid.

18 Theodore Gracyk, 'Having Bad Taste', *British Journal of Aesthetics*, XXX/2 (April 1990), p. 121.

19 Ibid., p. 126.

20 Dan Glaister, 'Thomas Kinkade: The Secret Life and Strange Death of Art's King of Twee', www.theguardian.com, 9 May 2012.

21 Kim Christensen, 'Dark Portrait of a "Painter of Light"', www.latimes.com, 5 March 2006.

22 Glaister, 'Thomas Kinkade'.

23 Biography, https://thomaskinkade.com, 1 February 2021.

24 *Bottle Shock*, www.quotes.net, accessed 1 April 2020.

25 Alexis Hartung, 'Factors Considered in Wine Evaluation', *Wine Society Journal*, XXXI/4 (Winter 1999).

26 Sylvia Wu, 'Chinese Wines Winning Seven Gold Medals Awarded Across Red, White, and Rosé', www.decanterchina.com, 28 May 2019.

27 Baggini, *The Virtues of the Table*, p. 219.

2 The Pleasures of Eating and Tasting

1 *Phaedo*, 60b.
2 Ibid.
3 *Gorgias*, 496e.
4 *Nicomachean Ethics*, 1152b1–4.
5 Ibid., 1152b20–24.
6 Augustine, *Confessions*, trans. R. S. Pine-Coffin (London, 1961), Book x, section 31.
7 Jeremy Bentham, *An Introduction to the Principles of Morals and Legislation*, ed. J. H. Burns and H.L.A. Hart, in *The Collected Works of Jeremy Bentham*, ed. J. H. Burns et al. (London and Oxford, 1970), p. 11.
8 Ibid., pp. 38–9.
9 John Stuart Mill, *Utilitarianism* (Indianapolis, IN, 2001), p. 4.
10 Ibid., p. 19.
11 Ibid.
12 Roger Scruton, *The Aesthetics of Architecture* (Princeton, NJ, 1979), p. 66.
13 Barbara Savedoff, 'Intellectual and Sensuous Pleasure', *Journal of Aesthetics and Art Criticism*, XLIII/3 (Spring 1985), p. 313.
14 Ibid., p. 314, my italics.
15 Ibid.
16 Isak Dinesen, 'Babette's Feast', in *Anecdotes of Destiny; and, Ehrengard* (New York, 1993), p. 16.
17 Ibid., p. 29.
18 Ibid.
19 Ibid., p. 41.
20 Denise Minger, *Death By Food Pyramid* (Malibu, CA, 2013) is a particularly interesting look at both the BMI and the history of the food pyramid.
21 Plato, *Republic*, Book 4.
22 Rudolph M. Bell, *Holy Anorexia* (Chicago, IL, 1987), p. 20.
23 International Dairy Foods Association, 'Ice Cream Sales and Trends', www.idfa.org, accessed 31 December 2019.
24 Jean Anthelme Brillat-Savarin, *The Physiology of Taste: Or Meditations on Transcendental Gastronomy*, trans. M.F.K. Fisher (New York, 1949), p. 15.
25 Kevin Melchionne, 'Artistic Dropouts', in *Aesthetics: The Big Questions*, ed. Carolyn Korsmeyer (Malden, MA, 1998), p. 101.
26 Ibid.

27 Ibid.
28 Ibid., pp. 101–2.

3 The Taste of Slow Food

1 Tom Mueller, *Extra Virginity: The Sublime and Scandalous World of Olive Oil* (New York, 2012), p. 96.
2 Carlo Petrini, *Slow Food: The Case for Taste* (New York, 2001), pp. xxiii–xxiv.
3 Ibid., p. 94.
4 Marc Lallanilla, 'Say Cheese! Roquefort May Keep Hearts Healthy', www.livescience.com, 17 December 2012; Ivan Petyaev et al., 'Roquefort Cheese Proteins Inhibit *Chlamydia pneumonia* Propagation and LPS-Induced Leukocyte Migration', *Scientific World Journal* (28 April 2013).
5 Michael Pollan, *In Defense of Food: An Eater's Manifesto* (New York, 2008).
6 Gregory Peterson, 'Is Eating Locally a Moral Obligation?', *Journal of Environmental Ethics*, 26 (2013), pp. 421–37.
7 Ibid., p. 428.
8 Petrini, *Slow Food*, p. 21.
9 Bill Nesto, 'Discovering Terroir in the World of Chocolate', *Gastronomica*, x/1 (Winter 2010), p. 131.
10 I had the great pleasure to spend a day at the Acetaia Leonardi balsamic production farm learning about this process: www.acetaialeonardi.it/en, accessed 23 February 2021.
11 The milk can come from either red cows, brown cows or Holsteins, but the red cows are by far the most prevalent.
12 Consorzio Vacche Rosse (Consortium of the Red Cow), 'The History of Parmesan Cheese (Parmigiano Reggiano), Our history', at www.consorziovaccherosse.it/en, accessed 10 March 2016.
13 Andrew Dalby, *Cheese: A Global History* (London, 2009), p. 9.
14 Esme Nicholson, 'Germany's Beer Purity Law Is 500 Years Old: Is It Past Its Sell-By Date?', www.npr.org, 29 April 2016.
15 Larry Olmsted, *Real Food/Fake Food: Why You Don't Know What You're Eating and What You Can Do About It* (Chapel Hill, NC, 2017).
16 Amy Trubeck, *The Taste of Place* (Berkeley, CA, 2008), p. 18.
17 Ibid.
18 Lisa Heldke, 'Down-Home Global Cooking: A Third Option Between Cosmopolitanism and Localism', in *A Philosophy of Food*, ed. David Kaplan (Berkeley, CA, 2012), p. 33.

19 Ibid., p. 37.
20 Ibid., p. 39.
21 Wendell Berry, *Bringing it to the Table: On Farming and Food* (Berkeley, CA, 2009), p. 227.
22 Pollan, *In Defense of Food*.
23 Berry, *Bringing it to the Table*, pp. 227–8.
24 Because of a law in the U.S. called the Country of Origin Labeling Program, which is enforced by the USDA, an Alaskan salmon, for instance, caught in U.S. waters off the coast of Alaska, will be processed in China. The labelling therefore must say that it is a product of China. For fish and shellfish, the method of production (wild or farmed) must also be labelled. With olive oil, although many brands (perhaps even most) advertise Italian olive oil, most labels now also reveal that although the oil was bottled in Italy (and thus a 'product of Italy'), the olive oil itself is from elsewhere, usually Spain, Greece or Argentina.
25 Berry, *Bringing it to the Table*, p. 229.
26 Adam Gopnik, *The Table Comes First: Family, France, and the Meaning of Food* (New York, 2012), p. 9.
27 Ibid.
28 Michael Pollan, *Cooked: A Natural History of Transformation* (New York, 2013).
29 Todd Kliman, 'How Michael Pollan, Alice Waters, and Slow Food Theorists Got It All Wrong: A Conversation with Food Historian (and Contrarian) Rachel Laudan', *The Washingtonian* (29 May 2015).
30 Rachel Laudan, 'A Plea for Culinary Modernism: Why We Should Love New, Fast, Processed Food', *Gastronomica*, I/1 (2001), pp. 36–44.
31 Kate Taylor, 'These 10 Companies Control Everything You Buy', *Business Insider* (4 April 2017). The companies are Unilever, Pepsi, Coca-Cola, Nestlé, Nabisco, General Mills, Mars and Dannon in the U.S.

4 Food Fraud and Authenticity

1 Walter Benjamin, 'The Work of Art in the Age of Mechanical Reproduction', in Benjamin, *Illuminations* (New York, 1968), pp. 217–51.
2 Hans Blumenberg, 'Light as a Metaphor for Truth: At the Preliminary Stage of Philosophical Concept Formation', in

Modernity and the Hegemony of Vision, ed. David Michael
Levin (Berkeley, CA, 1993), section 45.

3 Aristotle, *Metaphysics*, A. 980 a 25.

4 See Hans Jonas, 'The Nobility of Sight', *Philosophy and
Phenomenological Research*, 4 (June 1954), pp. 507–19.

5 Georg Hegel, *Aesthetics: Lectures on Fine Art*, trans. T. M. Knox
(Oxford, 1975), vol. I, p. 39.

6 Immanuel Kant, *Critique of the Power of Judgment*, ed. and trans.
Paul Guyer (New York, 2000), 14, 5:224.

7 Allen Carlson, 'Appreciation and the Natural Environment', *Journal
of Aesthetics and Art Criticism*, XXXVII (1979), p. 268.

8 Ibid., p. 271.

9 Ibid., p. 273.

10 Matteo Ravasio, 'Food Landscapes: An Object-Centered Model of
Food Appreciation', *The Monist* (2018), pp. 309–23.

11 Ibid., pp. 312–13.

12 Tom Mueller, *Extra Virginity: The Sublime and Scandalous World
of Olive Oil* (New York, 2012), p. 102.

13 Ibid., pp. 101–4.

14 Tom Mueller, 'Slippery Business: The Trade in Adulterated Olive
Oil', *New Yorker* (August 2007).

15 Larry Olmsted, *Real Food/Fake Food: Why You Don't Know What
You're Eating and What You Can Do About It* (Chapel Hill, NC,
2017), Ebook loc. 1381–2.

16 Mueller, 'Slippery Business'.

17 Ibid.

18 Mueller, *Extra Virginity*, p. 141.

19 Different accounts of this incident range from 600 deaths to
25,000. The discrepancy seems to come from deaths that happened
immediately and those subsequently thought to have been caused
by the bad oil. There are also clear indications of denial, cover-ups
and conspiracy theories as there really was so much on the line –
lives and olive oil. One account I read even went so far as to accuse
the tomato industry rather than allow the olive oil industry to take
the blame; Mueller, *Extra Virginity*, p. 110.

20 Ibid., p. 139.

21 Ibid.

22 Ibid., pp. 139–40.

23 Barry C. Smith, 'The Objectivity of Tastes and Tasting', in *Questions of
Taste: The Philosophy of Wine*, ed. Barry Smith (Oxford, 2007), p. 44.

24 Ibid., p. 62.

25 David Hume, 'Of the Standard of Taste', in *Essays Moral, Political, and Literary* (Indianapolis, IN, 1987), para. 3.

26 Ibid., para. 7.

27 Ibid.

28 Kant, *Critique of the Power of Judgment*, para. 7, 5, pp. 212–13, my italics.

29 Ibid., p. 356.

30 Ludwig Wittgenstein, *Philosophical Investigations*, trans. G.E.M. Anscombe (Oxford, 1997).

31 Aaron Meskin and Jon Robson, 'Taste and Acquaintance', *Journal of Aesthetics and Art Criticism*, LXXIII/2 (2015), p. 132.

32 Ibid., p. 132, my italics.

33 Ibid., my italics.

34 Frank Sibley, 'Tastes, Smells, and Aesthetics', in *Approaches to Aesthetics: Collected Papers on Philosophical Aesthetics*, ed. Frank Sibley (Oxford, 2001), p. 214.

35 Ibid.

5 Food Porn and the Power of Images

1 F. L. Fowler, *Fifty Shades of Chicken: A Parody in a Cookbook* (New York, 2012), p. 71.

2 Ibid., p. 8.

3 378 U.S. at 197 (Stewart, J., concurring).

4 Both Immanuel Kant (in the *Critique of Judgment*) and David Hume (in *Of the Standard of Taste*) talked about disinterestedness as an aesthetic goal with which we best consider art objects. This became a typical standard in eighteenth-century aesthetics, and for some time after that. Twentieth-century accounts do not necessarily consider this to be necessary, but it has become a touchstone in aesthetic theory and needs always to be referenced.

5 Alexander Cockburn, 'Gastro-Porn', *New York Review of Books* (8 December 1977), pp. 15–19.

6 Ibid., p. 8.

7 Ibid.

8 Yasmin Fahr, 'Food Porn Q&A with Amanda Simpson', www.thedailymeal.com, November 2010.

9 Urban Dictionary, 'Food Porn', www.urbandictionary.com, accessed 30 January 2021.

10 Thi Nguyen and Bekka Williams, 'Why We Call Things Porn',
    New York Times (26 July 2019).
11 Ibid.
12 Mary Devereaux, 'Oppressive Texts, Resisting Readers, and the
    Gendered Spectator: The "New" Aesthetics', in *Feminism and
    Tradition in Aesthetics*, ed. Peggy Brand and Carolyn Korsmeyer
    (University Park, PA, 1995), p. 126.
13 Laura Mulvey, 'Visual Pleasure and Narrative Cinema', *Screen*,
    XVI/3 (1975), pp. 6–18.
14 Erin Metz McDonnell, 'Food Porn: The Conspicuous Consumption
    of Food in the Age of Digital Reproduction', in *Food, Media, and
    Contemporary Culture: The Edible Image*, ed. Peri Bradley
    (New York, 2016), p. 257.
15 Ibid.
16 There has been much research on the relationship between men
    and meat: Carol Adams in *The Sexual Politics of Meat* (New York,
    2000); Matthew Ruby and Steven Heine, 'Meat, Morals, and
    Masculinity', *Appetite*, LVI (2011), pp. 447–50.
17 'Pro-ana' websites are generally locked so browsers and trolls
    cannot easily critique this 'lifestyle'.
18 Rosalind Coward, *Female Desire: Women's Sexuality Today*
    (London, 1984), p. 105.
19 Ibid., p. 103.
20 Ruby and Heine, 'Meat, Morals, and Masculinity', p. 447.
21 Guiltfree food, 3, www.adsoftheworld.com, September 2015.
22 Coward, *Female Desire*, p. 103.
23 Ibid.
24 John Wesley, *Primitive Physic; or, an Easy and Natural Method of
    Curing Most Diseases* [1847], https://thornber.net/medicine/html/
    primitive_printable.pdf, accessed 5 February 2020.
25 Rachel Hope Cleves, '"Those Dirty Words": Women,
    Pleasure, and the History of Food Porn', in *Food Porn*, Global
    Humanities 6, ed. Francesco Mangiapane and Frank Jacob
    (Bodø, 2019), p. 11.
26 Ibid.
27 Ibid., p. 13.
28 See Harvey Levenstein, 'Autointoxication and Its Discontents',
    in Levenstein, *Fear of Food: A History of Why We Worry about
    What We Eat* (Chicago, IL, 2012).
29 Kenneth Bendiner, *Food in Painting: From the Renaissance
    to the Present* (London, 2004), p. 134.

30 Edward Bullough, 'Psychical Distance as a Factor in Art and Aesthetic Principle', *British Journal of Psychology*, v (1912), p. 116.

31 Hans Maes, 'Who Says Pornography Can't Be Art?', in *Art and Pornography: Philosophical Essays*, ed. Hans Maes and Jerrold Levinson (Oxford, 2012).

32 Brian Wansink, Anupama Mukund and Andrew Weislogel, 'Food Art Does Not Reflect Reality: A Quantitative Content Analysis of Meals in Popular Paintings', *SAGE Open* (July–September 2016), p. 6.

33 Jon Simpson, 'Finding Brand Success in the Digital World', www.forbes.com, 25 August 2017.

34 *Republic*, 595b3–6, in *The Collected Dialogues of Plato*, ed. Edith Hamilton and Huntington Cairns (Princeton, NJ, 1961).

35 Jean Baudrillard, 'Simulacra and Simulations', in *Jean Baudrillard: Selected Writings*, ed. Mark Poster (Stanford, CA, 1988).

36 Ibid., p. 166.

37 Ibid., my italics.

38 Megan Garber, 'In Defense of Instagramming Your Food', *The Atlantic* (29 January 2016).

39 Ibid.

6 On Recipes and Rule Following

1 Michael Pollan, *In Defense of Food: An Eater's Manifesto* (New York, 2008), p. 3.

2 Massimo Montanari, *Food Is Culture*, trans. Albert Sonnenfeld (New York, 2006), p. xi.

3 Lisa Heldke, 'Recipes for Theory Making', *Hypatia*, III/2 (Summer 1988), pp. 15–29.

4 Plato, *Gorgias*, 462e.

5 Ibid., 463b1.

6 Alfred North Whitehead famously claimed that 'the safest general characterization of the European philosophical tradition is that it consists of a series of footnotes to Plato', *Process and Reality* (New York, 1979), p. 39.

7 We do know *something* about ancient Greek and Roman cooking. See, for instance, Eugenia Salza Prina Ricotti, *Meals and Recipes from Ancient Greece* (Los Angeles, CA, 2007), and Marcus Gavius Apicius, *Apicius*, the sole remaining cookbook from ancient Rome, ed. Sally Grainger, trans. Christopher Grocock (London, 2006).

8 Richard Parry, '*Episteme* and *Techne*', in *Stanford Encyclopedia of Philosophy*, ed. Edward N. Zalta (Summer 2020 edn), https://plato. stanford.edu.

9 Terry Nardin, 'Michael Oakeshott', in *Stanford Encyclopedia of Philosophy*, ed. Edward N. Zalta (Spring 2020 edn), https://plato. stanford.edu.

10 This is the ancient Greek *techne* and *phronesis* as outlined in Aristotle's *Nichomachean Ethics*, 1142a.

11 Immanuel Kant, *Critique of Pure Reason* (1793), 8:275.

12 Nardin, 'Michael Oakeshott'.

13 Rick Bragg, *The Best Cook in the World: Tales from My Momma's Table* (New York, 2018).

14 Emily Post, *Etiquette* (New York, 1922).

15 Bragg, *The Best Cook in the World*.

16 Ibid., pp. 14–15.

17 Ibid., p. 15.

18 Ibid., p. 16.

19 Fannie Merritt Farmer, *The Boston Cooking-School Cookbook* (Boston, MA, 1911), p. 25.

20 Ibid., italics in the original.

21 Bee Wilson, *Consider the Fork: A History of How We Cook and Eat* (New York, 2012), p. 126.

22 Polly Frost, 'Julia Child', www.interviewmagazine.com, 16 July 2009.

23 Court of Justice of the European Union PRESS RELEASE No. 171/18, 'The taste of a food product is not eligible for copyright protection', https://curia.europa.eu/jcms/upload/docs/application/pdf/2018-11/ cp180171en.pdf, 13 November 2018.

24 U.S. Copyright Office, Circular 33: 'Works Not Protected by Copyright', www.copyright.gov, accessed 10 April 2020.

25 Stephanie Smith, 'Food Network's "Dessert First" Star Axed in Recipe-Copy Flap: Sources', https://nypost.com, 16 February 2012.

26 Ian Harrison, 'Did Danny St-Pierre Just Apologize to SoupeSoup Boss Caroline Dumas?', https://montreal.eater.com, 19 February 2015.

27 Jonathan Bailey, 'Recipes, Copyright and Plagiarism', www. plagiarismtoday.com, 24 March 2015.

28 Nigella Lawson, *How to Eat: The Pleasures and Principles of Good Food* (New York, 2010).

29 Ibid.

30 Ibid.

31 Nigella Lawson, *How to Be a Domestic Goddess*, www.nigella.com, accessed 10 April 2020.

32 Martha Stewart, *Entertaining* (New York, 1982), p. 132.

33 Irma Rombauer and Marion Rombauer Becker, *Joy of Cooking* (New York, 1973), foreword.

34 Helen Rosner, 'The Strange, Uplifting Tale of "Joy of Cooking" Versus the Food Scientist', www.newyorker.com, 21 March 2018.

35 Henry Notaker, *A History of Cookbooks: From Kitchen to Page over Seven Centuries* (Oakland, CA, 2017).

36 Academia Barilla, 'On Honest Indulgence and Good Health', www.academiabarilla.it, accessed 22 April 2020.

37 Ibid.

38 Emilio Faccioli, *L'Arte della cucina in Italia* (Milan, 1987).

39 NESCO, 'Mediterranean Diet', www.unesco.org, accessed 14 February 2021.

40 Lydia Marie Gurney, *Things Mother Used to Make: A Collection of Ole Time Recipes, Some Nearly One Hundred Years Old and Never Published Before* (New York, 1922).

41 Karen Pinchin, 'How Slaves Shaped American Cooking: Slaves Planted the Seeds of Favorite Foods They Were Forced to Leave Behind', *National Geographic*, www.nationalgeographic.com, 1 March 2014.

42 Junior League of Montgomery, *Southern Recipes*, https://archive. org, accessed 14 February 2021.

43 Paula Deen, 'Bobby's Lighter Recipes: 6 Lighter Southern Recipes', www.pauladeen.com, accessed 16 May 2020.

44 Heldke, 'Recipes for Theory Making', p. 15.

45 Ibid., p. 16.

46 Ibid., p. 17.

47 Ibid.

48 John Dewey, *Logic: The Theory of Inquiry* (New York, 1938), pp. 104–5.

49 Heldke, 'Recipes for Theory Making', p. 21.

50 Wendell Berry, 'The Pleasures of Eating', in Berry, *What Are People For?* (New York, 1990).

Bibliography

Alexander, Kevin, 'Why "Authentic" Food is Bullshit', www.thrillist.com, 15 July 2016

Aristotle, *The Complete Works of Aristotle*

Aronson, Alex, 'The Anatomy of Taste', *Modern Language Notes*, LXI/4 (April 1946), pp. 228–36

Augustine, *Confessions*, trans. R. S. Pine-Coffin (London, 1961)

Baggini, Julian, *The Virtues of the Table: How to Eat and Think* (London, 2014)

Bailey, Andrew, *First Philosophy: Fundamental Problems and Readings in Philosophy* (Peterborough, ON, 2011)

Baldwin, Bird T., 'John Locke's Contributions to Education', *Sewanee Review*, XXI/2 (1913), pp. 177–87, www.jstor.org/stable/27532614

Baudrillard, Jean, 'Simulacra and Simulations', in *Jean Baudrillard: Selected Writings*, ed. Mark Poster (Stanford, CA, 1988), pp. 166–84

Baumgarten, Alexander, *Metaphysics*, trans. Courtney D. Fugate and John Hymers (London, 2013)

Bell, Rudolph M., *Holy Anorexia* (Chicago, IL, 1987)

Bendiner, Kenneth, *Food in Painting: From the Renaissance to the Present* (London, 2004)

Benjamin, Walter, 'The Work of Art in the Age of Mechanical Reproduction', in Benjamin, *Illuminations* (New York, 1968), pp. 217–51

Bentham, Jeremy, *An Introduction to the Principles of Morals and Legislation*, ed. J. H. Burns and H.L.A. Hart, in *The Collected Works of Jeremy Bentham*, ed. J. H. Burns et al. (London and Oxford, 1970)

Berkeley, George, *A Treatise Concerning the Principles of Human Knowledge* [1710] (Indianapolis, IN, 1982)

Berry, Wendell, *Bringing it to the Table: On Farming and Food* (Berkeley, CA, 2009)

——, 'The Pleasures of Eating', in Berry, *What are People For?* (New York, 1990)

Blumenberg, Hans, 'Light as a Metaphor for Truth: At the Preliminary
    Stage of Philosophical Concept Formation', in *Modernity and the
    Hegemony of Vision*, ed. David Michael Levin (Berkeley, CA, 1993),
    pp. 30–62
Borghini, Andrea, 'What is a Recipe?', *Journal of Agricultural and
    Environmental Ethics*, XXVIII (2015), pp. 719–38
Bourdieu, Pierre, 'From *Distinction*', in *Aesthetics: The Big Questions*,
    ed. Carolyn Korsmeyer (Malden, MA, 1998), pp. 150–55
Bragg, Rick, *The Best Cook in the World: Tales from My Momma's Table*
    (New York, 2018)
Brillat-Savarin, Jean Anthelme, *The Physiology of Taste: Or Meditations
    on Transcendental Gastronomy*, trans. M.F.K. Fisher (New York,
    1949)
Bullough, Edward, 'Psychical Distance as a Factor in Art and Aesthetic
    Principle', *British Journal of Psychology*, V (1912), pp. 87–117
Carlson, Allen, 'Appreciation and the Natural Environment',
    Journal of Aesthetics and Art Criticism, XXXVII (1979), pp. 267–75
Classen, Constance, *Worlds of Sense: Exploring the Senses in History
    and Across Cultures* (New York, 1993)
—, 'The Senses', in *Encyclopedia of European Social History*, vol. IV,
    ed. Peter Stearns (New York, 2001)
Cleves, Rachel Hope, '"Those Dirty Words": Women, Pleasure, and the
    History of Food Porn', in *Food Porn*, Global Humanities 6,
    ed. Francesco Mangiapane and Frank Jacob (Oslo, 2019)
Cockburn, Alexander, 'Gastro-Porn', *New York Review of Books*
    (8 December 1977), pp. 15–19
Coward, Rosalind, *Female Desire: Women's Sexuality Today* (London, 1984)
Dalby, Andrew, *Cheese: A Global History* (London, 2009)
Dennett, Daniel, *Consciousness Explained* (New York, 1991)
Descartes, Rene, *Meditations on First Philosophy in which the Existence
    of God and the Distinction between Soul and Body is Demonstrated*,
    3rd edn, trans. Donald Cress (Indianapolis, IN, 1993)
Devereaux, Mary, 'Oppressive Texts, Resisting Readers, and the
    Gendered Spectator: The "New" Aesthetics', in *Feminism and
    Tradition in Aesthetics*, ed. Peggy Brand and Carolyn Korsmeyer
    (University Park, PA, 1995), pp. 121–41
Dinesen, Isak, 'Babette's Feast', in *Anecdotes of Destiny; and, Ehrengard*
    (New York, 1993)
Freeland, Cynthia, 'Aristotle on the Sense of Touch', in *Essays on
    Aristotle's 'De Anima'*, ed. Martha C. Nussbaum and Amelie
    Oksenberg Rorty (Oxford, 2003), pp. 227–48

Ganson, Todd Stuart, 'The Platonic Approach to Sense-Perception', *History of Philosophy Quarterly*, xxii/1 (2005), pp. 1–15

Garber, Megan, 'In Defense of Instagramming Your Food', *The Atlantic* (29 January 2016)

Gopnik, Adam, *The Table Comes First: Family, France, and the Meaning of Food* (New York, 2012)

Gracyk, Theodore, 'Having Bad Taste', *British Journal of Aesthetics*, xxx/2 (April 1990), pp. 117–31

Hanna, Robert, and Monima Chadha, 'Non-Conceptualism and the Problem of Perceptual Self-Knowledge', *European Journal of Philosophy*, 11/19 (2011), pp. 184–223

Hegel, Georg, *Aesthetics: Lectures on Fine Art*, trans. T. M. Knox (Oxford, 1975), vol. i

Heldke, Lisa, 'Down-Home Global Cooking: A Third Option Between Cosmopolitanism and Localism', in *A Philosophy of Food*, ed. David Kaplan (Berkeley, CA, 2012), pp. 33–51

——, 'Recipes for Theory Making,' *Hypatia*, iii/2 (Summer 1988), pp. 15–29

Herder, Johann Gottfried von, 'On the Change of Taste' [1766], in *Herder: Philosophical Writings*, ed. Michael Forster (Cambridge, 2002), pp. 247–56

Howes, David, *The Sixth Sense Reader* (New York, 2009)

Hughes, Howard C., *Sensory Exotica: A World Beyond Human Experience* (Cambridge, MA, 2001)

Hume, David, 'Of The Standard of Taste', in *Essays Moral, Political, and Literary* (Indianapolis, IN, 1987), pp. 226–9

Jonas, Hans, 'The Nobility of Sight', *Philosophy and Phenomenological Research*, 4 (June 1954), pp. 507–19

Julier, Alice, *Eating Together: Food, Friendship, and Inequality* (Urbana, IL, 2013)

Jütte, Robert, *A History of the Senses: From Antiquity to Cyberspace*, trans. James Lynn (Cambridge, 2005)

Kant, Immanuel, *Critique of the Power of Judgment*, ed. and trans. Paul Guyer (New York, 2000), para 7, 5:212–13

——, *Groundwork of the Metaphysics of Morals*, trans. H. J. Patton (New York, 1964)

——, *Lectures on Ethics*, 'Of the Duties to the Body in Regard to the Sexual Impulse', ed. Peter Heath and J. B. Schneewind (Cambridge, 1997)

Kirk, G. S., and J. E. Raven, *The Presocratic Philosophers* (Cambridge, 1971)

Kliman, Todd, 'How Michael Pollan, Alice Waters, and Slow Food
     Theorists Got It All Wrong: A Conversation with Food Historian
     (and Contrarian) Rachel Laudan', *The Washingtonian* (29 May 2015)
Korsmeyer, Carolyn, 'Delightful, Delicious, Disgusting', *Journal of
     Aesthetics and Art Criticism*, LX/3 (2002), pp. 217–25
—, *Making Sense of Taste: Food and Philosophy* (Ithaca, NY, 1999)
Laudan, Rachel, 'A Plea for Culinary Modernism: Why We Should Love
     New, Fast, Processed Food', *Gastronomica*, I/1 (2001), pp. 36–44
—, 'Slow Food: The French Terroir Strategy, and Culinary Modernism',
     Food, Culture & Society, VII/2 (2004), pp. 133–44
Lawson, Nigella, *How to Eat: The Pleasures and Principles of Good Food*
     (New York, 2010)
—, *How to Be a Domestic Goddess*, www.nigella.com/books
Levenstein, Harvey, *Fear of Food: A History of Why We Worry about
     What We Eat* (Chicago, IL, 2012)
Levinovitz, Alan, *The Gluten Lie: And Other Myths about What You
     Eat* (New York, 2015)
Locke, John, *An Essay Concerning Human Understanding* [1698],
     ed. Peter Nidditch (Oxford, 1974)
McDonnell, Erin Metz, 'Food Porn: The Conspicuous Consumption
     of Food in the Age of Digital Reproduction', in *Food, Media, and
     Contemporary Culture: The Edible Image*, ed. Peri Bradley (New
     York, 2016), pp. 239–65
Maes, Hans, 'Who Says Pornography Can't Be Art?', in *Art and
     Pornography: Philosophical Essays*, ed. Hans Maes and Jerrold
     Levinson (Oxford, 2012)
Melchionne, Kevin, 'Acquired Taste', *Contemporary Aesthetics*, V
     (2007)
—, 'Artistic Dropouts', in *Aesthetics: The Big Questions*, ed. Carolyn
     Korsmeyer (Malden, MA, 1998), pp. 98–103
—, 'Norms of Cultivation', *Contemporary Aesthetics*, XIII (2015)
Meskin, Aaron, et al., 'Mere Exposure to Bad Art', *British Journal
     of Aesthetics*, LIII/2 (April 2013), pp. 139–64
Meskin, Aaron, and Jon Robson, 'Taste and Acquaintance', *Journal
     of Aesthetics and Art Criticism*, LXXIII/2 (2015), pp. 127–39
Mill, John Stuart, *Utilitarianism* (Indianapolis, IN, 2001)
Montanari, Massimo, *Cheese, Pears and History in a Proverb*,
     trans. Beth Archer Brombert (New York, 2010)
—, *Food Is Culture*, trans. Albert Sonnenfeld (New York, 2006)
Mueller, Tom, 'Slippery Business: The Trade in Adulterated
     Olive Oil', *New Yorker* (August, 2007)

——, *Extra Virginity: The Sublime and Scandalous World of Olive Oil*
(New York, 2012)

Mulvey, Laura, 'Visual Pleasure and Narrative Cinema', *Screen*, XVI/3
(1975), pp. 6–18

Nesto, Bill, 'Discovering Terroir in the World of Chocolate',
Gastronomica, X/1 (Winter 2010), pp. 131–5

Nguyen, Thi, and Bekka Williams, 'Why We Call Things Porn', *New York
Times* (26 July 2019)

Nicholson, Esme, 'Germany's Beer Purity Law Is 500 Years Old.
Is It Past Its Sell-By Date?' www.npr.org, 29 April 2016

Olmsted, Larry, *Real Food/Fake Food: Why You Don't Know What You're
Eating and What You Can Do About It* (Chapel Hill, NC, 2017)

Perullo, Nicola, 'On the Correspondence Between Visual and
Gustatory Perception', in *Taste*, ed. Andrea Pavoni et al.
(London, 2018), pp. 175–92

Peterson, Gregory, 'Is Eating Locally a Moral Obligation?',
Journal of Environmental Ethics, 26 (2013), pp. 421–37

Petrini, Carlo, *Slow Food: The Case for Taste* (New York, 2003)

——, *Slow Food Nation* (New York, 2013)

Plato, *The Collected Dialogues of Plato*, ed. Edith Hamilton and
Huntington Cairns (Princeton, NJ, 1961)

Pollan, Michael, *In Defense of Food: An Eater's Manifesto* (New York,
2008)

Ravasio, Matteo, 'Food Landscapes: An Object-Centered Model of Food
Appreciation', *The Monist* (2018), pp. 309–23

Ray, Krishnendu, 'Domesticating Cuisine: Food and Aesthetics
on American Television', *Gastronomica*, VII/1 (Winter 2007),
pp. 50–63

Rudinow, Joel, 'Race, Ethnicity, Expressive Authenticity: Can White
People Sing the Blues?', *Journal of Aesthetics and Art Criticism*,
LII/1 (1994), pp. 127–37

Savedoff, Barbara, 'Intellectual and Sensuous Pleasure', *Journal of
Aesthetics and Art Criticism*, XLIII/3 (Spring 1985), pp. 313–15

Scruton, Roger, *The Aesthetics of Architecture* (Princeton, NJ, 1979)

——, 'Architectural Taste', *British Journal of Aesthetics*, XV
(Autumn 1975), pp. 294–328

Sheldrake, Rupert, 'The Sense of Being Stared At', in *The Sixth
Sense Reader*, ed. David Howes (New York, 2009)

Sibley, Frank, 'Tastes, Smells, and Aesthetics', in *Approaches to
Aesthetics: Collected Papers on Philosophical Aesthetics*,
ed. Frank Sibley (Oxford, 2001)

Smith, Barry C., 'The Objectivity of Tastes and Tasting', in *Questions of Taste: The Philosophy of Wine*, ed. Barry Smith (Oxford, 2007), pp. 41–77

Solomon, Robert, 'On Kitsch and Sentimentality', *Journal of Aesthetics and Art Criticism*, XLIX/1 (Winter 1991), pp. 1–14

Sorabji, Richard, 'Aristotle on Demarcating the Five Senses', *Philosophical Review*, LXXX/1 (1971), pp. 55–79

Stewart, Martha, *Entertaining* (New York, 1982)

Stiles, Kaelyn, Ozlem Altok and Michael Bell, 'The Ghosts of Taste: Food and the Cultural Politics of Authenticity', *Agriculture and Human Values*, XXVIII/2 (2011), pp. 225–36

Trubeck, Amy, *The Taste of Place* (Berkeley, CA, 2008)

Varga, Somogy, and Charles Guignon, 'Authenticity', in *Stanford Encyclopedia of Philosophy* (2014), at www.plato.stanford.edu

Wansink, Brian, Anupama Mukund and Andrew Weislogel, 'Food Art Does Not Reflect Reality: A Quantitative Content Analysis of Meals in Popular Paintings', *SAGE Open* (July–September 2016), pp. 1–10

Waterfield, Robin, ed., *The First Philosophers: The Presocratics and the Sophists* (Oxford, 2000)

Wilson, Bee, *Consider the Fork: A History of How We Cook and Eat* (New York, 2012)

Wittgenstein, Ludwig, *Philosophical Investigations*, trans. G.E.M. Anscombe (Oxford, 1997)

Acknowledgements

I became interested in food as an academic discipline when I had kids (twin boys who are now fourteen). Reading about what I should feed them ended up in a Philosophy of Food class that my department chair at the time, David Shaner, allowed me to teach without question. He always took the attitude that we should teach what we were excited about, since the students would always see that excitement. Because I work at an amazing university, I was able to add to that class a 'food lab' taught by the head chef for the university, Chef Ralph Macrina. Chef Ralph taught me to cook beyond what I thought possible, and shared with me and countless students his absolute passion for and dedication to food. I do not know a harder-working person at the university. Thanks to Aramark and now *Bon Appetit* for their support of my Philosophy of Food class.

Not long after I started teaching that class, I was invited to lead a study-away programme to Italy to teach students about the Italian Slow Food movement. There I was able to work with Antonello Siragusa, his parents Giuseppe and Maria, and all of the wonderful people who worked at Italy Farm Stay in Sora. I had the absolute pleasure of leading this trip with my colleagues, 'Lucky' Lloyd Benson and 'Professor Peacock' Bill Allen. I ate delicious food, I became reconnected to the land and learned how to make pasta, gnocchi, bread, cheese, olive oil and wine, among other things. We learned where our meat came from in the most literal sense, hiked, ate, played cards and laughed a lot. The students on those trips were (mostly) wonderful, and I was glad to have such great travel companions and dinner companions. Ben Davids, Jesse Tompkins and Morgan Cooper were students who travelled to Italy with me in different years, and who have all now become friends and dinner companions. They have all read chapters of this book and given me helpful feedback.

Rafe McGregor read a draft of the whole book and gave me extremely helpful feedback. Darren Hick, Eva Dadlez, Eileen John and Sarah Archino all read chapters and helped me to craft more interesting examples, more engaging prose and more real-life problems to examine. James C. Edwards, my teacher, colleague, mentor and friend, read early drafts, but passed away before I completed the final draft. He is missed dearly, but his impact will be felt for a long time by me and many others.

Finally I must thank my husband, Bill, and my boys, William and Charles. Bill has supported all of my travels, cooking experiments, excessive book purchases and more discussions about food and eating than he ever anticipated. He has always been a willing companion and participant, and he has supported me unconditionally in my quests to cook better, to try different foods, to travel anywhere, and to welcome people to our dinner table as the most gracious host. My life has benefited in countless ways from his love.

Index